# The Soviet Union
## and
## Ballistic Missile Defense

The Johns Hopkins Foreign Policy Institute (FPI) was founded in 1980 and serves as the research center for the School of Advanced International Studies (SAIS) in Washington, D.C. The FPI is a meeting place for SAIS faculty members and students as well as for government analysts, policymakers, diplomats, journalists, business leaders, and other specialists in international affairs. In addition to conducting research on policy-related international issues, the FPI sponsors conferences, seminars, and roundtables.

The FPI's research activities are often carried out in conjunction with SAIS's regional and functional programs dealing with Latin America and the Caribbean Basin, U.S. foreign policy, U.S.-Japan relations, Canada, Africa, Europe, security studies, international energy, and international economics.

FPI publications include the *SAIS Review*, a biannual journal of foreign affairs, which is edited by SAIS students; the SAIS Papers in International Affairs, a monograph series copublished with Westview Press in Boulder, Colorado; the FPI Policy Briefs, a series of analyses of immediate or emerging foreign-policy issues; and the FPI Case Studies, a series designed to teach analytical negotiating skills.

*The Soviet Union and Ballistic Missile Defense* is the third in a series of five books. This series is being prepared by the FPI as part of a research project on the long-term implications of military programs and activities in space for strategic stability, superpower relations, and alliance cohesion.

For additional information regarding FPI publications, write to: FPI Publications Program, School of Advanced International Studies, The Johns Hopkins University, 1740 Massachusetts Avenue, N.W., Washington, D.C. 20036.

# ABOUT THE BOOK AND AUTHOR

In the recent debate over strategic defense, the Soviet dimension has not been adequately examined. Dr. Parrott's multifaceted discussion of the Soviet approach to ballistic missile defense (BMD) admirably fills that gap. Based on an analysis of Soviet statements and Soviet weaponry, the study surveys Soviet perceptions of the shifting relationship between the superpowers and the effect of BMD on that relationship. The author then traces the evolution of Soviet policies toward ballistic missile defense and the introduction of weapons into space. After exploring the internal budgetary debates that will affect future Soviet decisions on BMD and space systems, the book outlines Soviet responses, political as well as military, to the Strategic Defense Initiative and concludes with recommendations for U.S. policy toward BMD and arms negotiations.

Bruce Parrott is the director of Soviet Studies at The Johns Hopkins School of Advanced International Studies. He is the author of *Politics and Technology in the Soviet Union* (1983) and editor of *Trade, Technology, and Soviet-American Relations* (1985). He is currently writing a book on the politics of Soviet defense spending.

# SAIS
# PAPERS IN INTERNATIONAL AFFAIRS

# The Soviet Union
# and
# Ballistic Missile Defense

## Bruce Parrott

WESTVIEW PRESS/BOULDER AND LONDON
WITH THE FOREIGN POLICY INSTITUTE
SCHOOL OF ADVANCED INTERNATIONAL STUDIES
THE JOHNS HOPKINS UNIVERSITY

*A Westview Press / Foreign Policy Institute Edition*

Published in 1987 in the United States of America by Westview Press, Inc.; Frederick A. Praeger, Publisher; 5500 Central Avenue, Boulder, Colorado 80301

Library of Congress Catalog Card Number: 86-51633
ISBN 0-8133-7429-4

Composition for this book was provided by The Magazine Group, Inc., Washington, D.C., for The Johns Hopkins Foreign Policy Institute, SAIS.
This book was produced without formal editing by the publisher.

Printed and bound in the United States of America

The paper used in this publication meets the requirements of the American National Standard for Permanence of Paper for Printed Library Materials Z39.48-1984.

6    5    4    3    2

Dedicated with all my love
to Sindy and Matthew,
who lived through it,
and to Lydia,
who cleverly arrived
in time to celebrate

# CONTENTS

*Acknowledgments*    *xi*

1. The Central Issues                                                    *1*

2. Soviet Views of the Geopolitical Context                              *9*

3. Soviet Policy Toward Soviet BMD
   and the Military Uses of Space                                       *23*

4. The Resource Allocation Debate and Soviet
   BMD Decisions                                                        *45*

5. Soviet Responses to the Strategic Defense
   Initiative                                                           *53*

6. U.S. Policy and the Future of the Superpower
   Arms Competition                                                     *81*

*Notes*    *93*

# ACKNOWLEDGMENTS

This book is one of several studies prepared for a project on "The Military Uses of Space." Funded by the Carnegie Corporation of New York, the project is being conducted under the auspices of the Foreign Policy Institute of The Johns Hopkins University School of Advanced International Studies.

In writing the book I have received generous help from several persons. I want especially to thank Harold Brown, chairman of the Foreign Policy Institute, and Simon Serfaty, the institute's executive director, for encouraging me to undertake the study and waiting patiently for its completion. Other scholars who read and commented on preliminary drafts include Charles Fairbanks, Douglas Garthoff, Raymond Garthoff, Lawrence Gershwin, David Holloway, Simon Kassel, Glenn Kent, Stanley Kober, Michael MccGwire, Gordon Schloming, Helmut Sonnenfeldt, Paul Stares, and Edward Warner III. None of these experts would agree with everything the book contains, and a few would probably differ with its central thesis. But all have helped make it better than it otherwise could have been.

In addition, I wish to express my appreciation to the Woodrow Wilson International Center for Scholars, where I completed the final draft of the book while a fellow. My thanks go as well to Andrew Kuchins, Anne Herr, and Stephen Foye for their assistance in locating elusive sources, and to Nancy McCoy for her sterling editing.

Finally, my family's contribution to the book deserves recognition. During the writing, Sindy Parrott, my wife, generously shouldered a disproportionate share of our household's daily tasks, despite her own demanding professional obligations. For this I owe her a special debt of gratitude. Help of a different sort came from Matthew, our five-year-old son, who praised books that tell a story and reminded me through his actions that life's meaning depends on play as well as work.

*Bruce Parrott*

# 1.
# THE CENTRAL ISSUES

In the recent American debate over strategic defense, the Soviet dimension of the problem has received little systematic attention. Although a substantial body of pertinent Western scholarship exists, public discussion of the Strategic Defense Initiative (SDI) has taken inadequate notice of Soviet views and policies.[1] A number of U.S. officials, omitting the Soviet perspective entirely or assuming that Soviet policy is already permanently fixed, have implicitly discounted the need to consider possible Soviet responses to new U.S. strategic undertakings.[2] More wisely, other observers have examined Soviet policy options, but they have focused primarily on the specific military programs the Soviets have already begun or might initiate if the United States continues a large effort meant to produce an extensive system of ballistic missile defense (BMD). Although necessary, such a focus on the technical dimension of Soviet policy neglects the vital question of how BMD fits into broader Soviet conceptions of international politics and military strategy. The limited number of U.S. commentators who have actually pursued this question, however, have frequently been so eager to use Soviet statements as ammunition in the American debate over SDI that they have made little effort to distinguish Soviet propaganda from real Soviet beliefs.[3]

The failure to devote sustained attention to the Soviet approach to ballistic missile defense is a critical deficiency of the Western public debate over U.S. policy. Without a careful effort to understand the strategic, political, and economic context of Soviet military choices, Western policymakers may seriously misjudge the current situation. For instance, U.S. officials, relying on statements of Soviet strategic doctrine formulated in the 1960s, have suggested that the USSR is already committed to deploying its own large-scale BMD system, whatever the United States may do.[4] But such references to supposedly "timeless" Soviet military doctrines are unreliable guides to contemporary Soviet policy. Insufficient attention to the evolution of Soviet doctrines on BMD invites anachronistic evaluations of current Soviet views and obscures the interaction between U.S. and Soviet strategic decisions.[5] Moreover, a narrow focus on Soviet military options neglects the nonmilitary factors, both economic and political, that may exert a decisive influence on Soviet policy toward strategic defense.[6] No less important, a "grab bag" approach to Soviet sources ignores the existence of Soviet debates over BMD and runs the risk of mistaking minority Soviet views for established policy.[7] Only careful sifting can distinguish the various strands of Soviet policy discourse and sort out real statements of policy from propaganda.

Distinguishing real from feigned Soviet beliefs is, of course, no easy matter. Western observers of Soviet military affairs differ over how to treat Soviet public statements and how to balance these statements against such observable Soviet behavior as weapons tests and deployments. This study is based on the assumption that both Soviet words and deeds are indispensable data for understanding Soviet conduct. Soviet weapons programs must be carefully analyzed to discern Soviet military capabilities and the possible range of Soviet strategic intentions. But Soviet statements must also be studied to understand the frequent cases in which these "hard" data do not resolve crucial questions about underlying Soviet military and political aims. In such cases, as Robert Tucker has astutely observed, Western debates about Soviet strategic intentions are at bottom disputes about the character of the Soviet regime.[8] The further ahead we try to see, the less conclusive becomes the evidence derived from existing Soviet military programs. In the long run, Western analysts must ask not simply, "What can the Soviets now do militarily?" but "What are the Soviets determined to be able to do in the future?"

Can useful insights into the USSR's real aims be gleaned from what the Soviets say? At first glance the pervasiveness of Soviet ideology and the heavy Soviet dependence on domestic and international propaganda suggest that the answer is no. In actuality, however, much can be learned from Soviet speeches and writings. To begin with, the party Politburo must explain its policies not only to foreign and domestic publics but also to other members of the elite. The Politburo can rely on subordinate political, military, and economic officials to implement its policies only if they understand those policies. The party leadership, for instance, cannot afford to mislead the officer corps about its real military policies by issuing military literature that consists solely of propaganda.[9] Even speeches and articles that are widely distributed at home and abroad often contain guidelines to policy, although these guidelines are commonly stated in veiled terms.[10] In addition, the regime issues many specialized books and periodicals, including foreign-policy and military journals, which are intended primarily for members of the domestic elite rather than for ordinary citizens or foreign audiences. These sources treat controversial issues more frankly and shed more light on operational Soviet policy than do mass-circulation publications.[11] Moreover, Western analysts can check some conclusions drawn from the open Soviet literature against the contents of military writings, particularly the General Staff journal *Military Thought*, which are prepared solely for the confidential use of Soviet officers rather than for publication. Scrutiny of these writings can give Western analysts a firmer grasp of real Soviet strategic thinking—thinking that, on the whole, has been mirrored in the specialized published literature.[12] Finally, despite the premium that official Soviet ideology places on public unanimity, the views expressed in Soviet publications sometimes contradict one another and occasionally spark open polemics. By examining these controversies, outside observers can gain further insight into the real issues occupying the attention of Soviet decisionmakers.

The remainder of this book is divided into five chapters. The study begins by analyzing Soviet views of the superpowers' shifting geopolitical relationship and BMD's impact on it. Against this backdrop, the following chapter traces the evolution of Soviet policies toward Soviet ballistic missile defense and the introduction of weapons into space.[13] Turning from the international to the domestic context, the study then explores the resource allocation debate that will affect future Soviet decisions on strategic defense and space systems. Next it outlines possible Soviet responses to the U.S. strategic defense program and examines the implications of SDI for Soviet policies toward arms control. The final chapter presents recommendations for U.S. policy toward BMD and arms negotiations.

The central propositions presented in the book are as follows:

- The possibility of an unregulated superpower race in BMD and space technologies is part of a larger set of recent international trends that Soviet decisionmakers find deeply unsettling. In Moscow these trends have raised serious doubts about the wisdom of Soviet external policy during the 1970s and have produced sharp internal differences over policy toward the United States. Already highly suspicious of the Reagan administration, the elite is united by a general conviction that SDI is a dangerous U.S. gambit that may ultimately undercut past Soviet strategic gains and pose a grave new threat to Soviet security. The elite is divided, however, by differences over the precise nature of the threat and how to cope with it.

- The USSR's policy toward its own strategic defense and military space programs has been prompted by diverse and sometimes contradictory goals. Although Soviet decisionmakers at first favored developing a large Soviet BMD system, in the late 1960s they reappraised this policy and began negotiating an antiballistic missile (ABM) treaty that sharply restricted Soviet BMD activities. One major reason the regime signed the 1972 ABM treaty was to reduce the chances of again falling behind the United States in an expanded arms race involving defensive as well as offensive weapons. A further reason was the belief, held by some but not all Soviet observers, that the accord would help stabilize superpower relations in times of crisis and thereby reduce the likelihood of nuclear war. After the signing of the treaty, a group within the military high command continued to voice arguments for the ultimate development and deployment of a large Soviet BMD system. However, although these proposals may have helped fuel the USSR's substantial program of BMD research and development, the notion of actually building a large BMD system has not been accepted by the party leadership.

- Apart from general considerations of strategic stability, powerful internal political and economic constraints have reinforced the party leadership's desire to avoid an all-out race in BMD and space weapons. Today the party chiefs recognize the technological weaknesses of their system far more clearly than they did when the ABM treaty was first signed, and they are already embroiled in internal controversies over the trade-offs among military and civilian programs. An all-out BMD competition would impose heavy new strains on the faltering economy and force extremely difficult political decisions on the leadership. For this reason, while the Air Defense Forces and parts of the General Staff may favor an all-out race against the United States in BMD and space weapons, the bulk of the party leadership and several military services are likely to strive to avoid it.

- Thanks to this combination of strategic assessments and domestic difficulties, the USSR's preferred response to SDI is political rather than military. In the next two or three years the regime will work assiduously to counter SDI by political means and will postpone the initiation of large new military undertakings. The key deadline for deciding on a major expansion of Soviet military programs will probably arrive shortly after the U.S. 1988 presidential elections, when it should become more evident whether SDI enjoys strong bipartisan support and when U.S. field tests and the Soviet military procurement cycle will increase the pressure for clear-cut policy decisions.

- If the U.S. commitment seems definite, the first Soviet military response will probably be to develop sophisticated antisatellite (ASAT) and other defense-suppression weapons and next to upgrade strategic offensive forces. Despite the mounting economic constraints on Soviet military spending, these responses are well within Soviet technical and industrial capabilities. The burden inflicted by the development and deployment of an extensive Soviet BMD system will be much greater. But if the SDI program moves into the stages of field testing and design, it is virtually certain that the USSR will also accelerate R and D on ballistic missile defense with the aim of ultimately deploying a similar system of its own.

- Because the Soviets fear it deeply, SDI has already exerted a profound effect on their attitudes toward arms control, and it will continue to do so. Whether this effect proves to be positive or negative will depend largely on U.S. policy. If the Soviets can obtain a firm U.S. commitment to postpone SDI testing and deployment and limit the United States' offensive nuclear arsenal, they will almost certainly agree to make deep cuts in their own nuclear weapons. If they are unable to obtain such an agreement directly, they may consider concluding other agreements in order to encourage a Western reappraisal of SDI. One possible alternative that the Soviets have already mooted is to decouple the issue of offensive intermediate-range nuclear weapons from SDI and sign a separate intermediate-range nuclear force (INF) accord. Another alternative might be to negotiate a new five- or ten-year ceiling on the growth of strategic offensive arsenals. However, internal political obstacles and the unpredictability of Western public opinion may cause the leadership to rule out the first alternative and are even more likely to sway it against the second. More improbable still is Soviet agreement to a permanent accord or to deep cuts in offensive weapons without firm guarantees against the early deployment of a large U.S. BMD system, because such agreements would limit Soviet military options for countering the system if it is deployed.

- Whatever specific military policies the Soviets settle on, they will put no faith in U.S. proposals for a negotiated joint transition to a world of space-based BMD. Instead, their strategic calculations are likely to lead them to adopt measures that will undermine rather than strengthen the national security of the United States. Soviet development and deployment of highly effective ASAT weapons would probably reduce the stability of the superpower relationship and, combined with Soviet strategic offensive arms, could easily leave the United States at a net military disadvantage. Moreover, while the United States may achieve a temporary monopoly on space-based BMD weaponry, this monopoly is unlikely to be permanent. U.S. policymakers should therefore consider very carefully whether it would be in the long-term American interest for the Soviet Union to possess such a system. Finally, they should carefully weigh the possibility, as yet hypothetical but nevertheless conceivable, that one unintended consequence of an all-out competition in BMD may be to endow the USSR with a dangerous new capacity to attack the United States directly from space.

# 2.
# SOVIET VIEWS OF THE
# GEOPOLITICAL CONTEXT

To understand Soviet policies toward ballistic missile defense and the military uses of space, we must begin by considering the overall context in which the Soviets evaluate trends in military relations between the superpowers. Although many Americans perceive the Strategic Defense Initiative and its motives separately from the broader pattern of superpower relations, the opposite is true of Soviet observers. Rather than view SDI as a novel undertaking motivated by a humanitarian impulse to reduce the risks of nuclear war, the Soviets regard it as an extension of the continuing geopolitical competition between the United States and the USSR. Their perceptions of general trends in the superpower competition profoundly affect their attitudes toward the Reagan administration's plans for strategic defense and the military uses of space. Whatever independent impulses the Soviets may have had to move in similar directions—and, as shown in the next chapter, they have had some impulses of this kind—we cannot understand their likely responses to U.S. initiatives without examining the broader international setting.

For the Soviets, the dominant international fact of the 1980s has been the geopolitical resurgence of the United States and the decline of superpower détente. Although the greater assertiveness of the United States strikes many Western observers as an inevitable consequence of Soviet actions during the 1970s, it has perplexed Soviet policymakers. During the 1970s they believed that they had discovered a workable formula for managing relations with the United States. As it crystallized during the late 1960s, the formula called for a steady expansion of Soviet military power to underwrite Soviet global influence and gain international standing as the United States' equal; the avoidance of superpower confrontations in central Europe and a new accent on diplomatic negotiations to reinforce Western groups favoring a conciliatory line toward the USSR; the conclusion of arms-control agreements that would codify Soviet strategic gains, reduce the likelihood of a new U.S. military buildup, and permit a slowing of the growth of the Soviet military effort; and low-risk steps to expand Soviet footholds in the Third World.

The inauguration of this combination of policies at the start of the 1970s generated conflict within the Soviet leadership. Politburo members Piotr Shelest and Aleksandr Shelepin, aided perhaps by other party leaders, resisted the shift toward détente with the West, particularly the conclusion of strategic arms-control agreements with the United States.[1] In 1975–76 there was a further, short-lived controversy when Brezhnev and his political allies trimmed the growth of the defense budget over the protests of Marshal A.A. Grechko, the minister of defense and a member of the Politburo.[2] As shown below, some military spokesmen also dissented from official BMD policy and lobbied for more vigorous research into possible future BMD systems.

Nonetheless, during the second half of the 1970s a policy consensus gradually took hold within the political elite. Shelest and Shelepin were removed from the Politburo in 1973 and 1975, respectively, and Marshal Grechko's death in 1976 paved the way for Dmitri Ustinov, Leonid Brezhnev's longtime political ally, to become defense minister. In the wake of these changes there were few signs of serious dissatisfaction within the military and foreign-policy establishments. By the late 1970s Brezhnev's mix of military power, arms negotiations, and diplomacy appeared to be yielding major benefits. Based on a combination of cooperation and competition with the West, his dual-track formula for détente helped consolidate the USSR's standing as a military superpower and produced major geopolitical gains in Europe and the Third World. Moreover, Brezhnev achieved these gains while satisfying the basic institutional and budgetary interests of most components of the elite. It is thus not surprising that conservative as well as ''liberal'' Soviet officials joined ranks behind Brezhnev's approach to détente. After some initial foot-dragging, for example, officers who had previously espoused hard-line military policies backed Brezhnev's 1977 declaration disavowing strategic superiority as a Soviet military goal,[3] and the controversy over BMD policy also subsided.

By the end of the decade, however, Soviet decisionmakers discovered that the dual-track formula for East-West détente was in danger of failure. During the late 1970s U.S. political circles, unaware of the slowdown in the growth of Soviet defense spending and alarmed by Soviet Third World ventures such as Angola and Afghanistan, became increasingly critical of the USSR. In the second half of the Carter presidency the U.S. defense budget, after declining for several years in real terms, began to increase. The United States, while refusing to ratify the SALT II treaty, joined its NATO allies in a tentative plan to counter new Soviet SS–20 rockets by deploying the sort of forward-based missiles in Europe that the USSR had reluctantly omitted from the treaty's coverage in order to gain U.S. approval of the treaty.[4]

Moreover, in 1980 Ronald Reagan was elected president on a party platform that explicitly called for the United States to regain military superiority over the USSR. Proclaiming that past strategic arms-control agreements had undermined U.S. security, President Reagan began talks with the Soviet Union over strategic and intermediate-range nuclear weapons only after domestic and West European political pressure for this step became intense, and he indicated a willingness to conclude new agreements only if they would improve the military balance in the United States' favor.[5] The Reagan administration evinced little interest in renewing the sets of bilateral negotiations over antisatellite weapons and over a comprehensive nuclear test ban that had begun under the Carter administration.[6] Meanwhile it enunciated a highly ambitious new military strategy and sharply accelerated the U.S. military buildup begun under president Carter. To Soviet observers, these steps made President Reagan's condemnation of the USSR as an ''evil empire'' seem like more than rhetoric.

It is true, of course, that other circumstances might have made the developments mentioned above appear less ominous from the Soviet perspective. The Reagan administration has carefully avoided direct military confrontations with the USSR. Since 1984 it has tempered the tone of its pronouncements about the Soviet regime, and it is still equivocating over whether permanently to breach the limits of the unratified SALT II agreement that it has disavowed. The administration's Soviet policy has also encountered periodic bouts of skepticism in Western Europe and rising political and budgetary pressures at home. However, while some Soviet officials have viewed these facts as significant, none has drawn much reassurance from them. Instead Kremlin decisionmakers have asked whether the Soviet policies of the 1970s were mistaken and whether the possibility of Soviet-American détente has been irretrievably lost.

Since about 1980 Soviet ruling circles have engaged in a running debate over this question. Although Western analysts have not yet pieced together all the fragments of the debate, some of its features can be discerned. Because it centers on the nature and management of the superpower relationship, this intramural discussion bears directly on how Soviet decisionmakers view the issue of BMD, including SDI, and how they appraise their own policy options in strategic defense.

In the past few years virtually all Soviet officials and specialists have accepted the idea that the United States is striving to reestablish a position of military superiority over the USSR and that the danger of war between the superpowers has increased. Every general secretary from Brezhnev through Gorbachev has affirmed this proposition.[7] However, Soviet foreign-policy experts have disagreed about the depth of U.S. hostility and about whether the Reagan administration and its successors will be able to muster the resources to sustain the push for superiority over the long haul. Some specialists, both military and civilian, have implied that the United States has launched an enduring drive for superiority that will block the achievement of new arms agreements for a long time, whereas other specialists have contended that domestic constraints and West European resistance will prevent the United States from attaining this goal and will facilitate the conclusion of new arms accords.[8]

Because the members of the Soviet elite differ over the political feasibility of the U.S. quest for superiority and the rapidity with which it might be achieved, they have favored divergent policy prescriptions. Broadly speaking, during the 1980s all party general secretaries have favored a similar course of action toward the United States. While inveighing against the U.S. quest for global primacy, each has expressed the belief that superpower détente can be revived and has favored an approach calculated to deflect the United States onto a less assertive path primarily through political means. From this perspective, the United States' new assertiveness can best be countered over the long term by following a patient strategy of political maneuver, public diplomacy, and substantive negotiations, rather than by engaging in an unregulated arms race or military confrontation.[9] Each of the top leaders has expressed a qualified hope that Western political groups favoring a more accommodating policy toward the USSR will gain renewed influence, thereby ensuring the ultimate triumph of "reason" in relations between the superpowers.[10]

A minority within the leadership, however, has dissented from this position. Backed by high-level party leaders, elements of the military high command have suggested that Soviet-American détente cannot be reestablished on acceptable terms, leaving no alternative except prolonged political hostility and an all-out arms race with the United States. In the early 1980s, for example, Marshal Nikolai Ogarkov, then first deputy minister of defense and chief of the General Staff, raised an open challenge to established party policy. Ogarkov claimed that the United States had embarked on an enduring quest for "overwhelming" military superiority and was striving to wreck past arms agreements and current arms-control negotiations. Despite the heightened Soviet public accent on the danger of nuclear war, Ogarkov claimed that party propaganda was still underestimating the military danger from the United States. Warning against "subjectivism" in appraising international military trends, he observed that such an underestimation of the danger of war might have "grave consequences" and called for a sharp acceleration of the development and deployment of Soviet weaponry.[11]

By 1984 Ogarkov, who repeatedly implied that Soviet diplomacy and arms-control negotiations were incapable of constraining the U.S. defense buildup, was hinting that failure to institute major new military programs would be a "serious mistake" that could jeopardize the power of the Soviet state.[12] Given the long-standing pattern of civilian control over the Soviet military establishment, it is inconceivable that the marshal could have openly challenged prevailing policy for so long without substantial support in top party echelons. Although sketchy, the evidence examined below indicates that Ogarkov may have received backing from such Politburo members as G.V. Romanov and V.V. Shcherbitskii.

The critics have buttressed their internal policy challenge with the claim that superpower détente is a relic of the past and cannot be restored. In 1983, for example, one Soviet defense analyst emphasized the exceptional practical importance of the military threat emanating from the West and voiced a belief that Western Europe could not be used as an effective check on such U.S. military plans as the forthcoming INF deployments. In the same vein, he proposed a periodization of postwar international relations into three stages—the first consisting of the cold war, the second of détente, and the third of the era of renewed hostility in the 1980s. Without disagreeing, this officer quoted the 1980 Republican party platform to the effect that détente "is dead."[13]

These hard-line sentiments have gathered enough support within the Soviet elite that the proponents of détente have felt compelled to reply publicly. For example, soon after Ogarkov began to voice his criticism, an editorial in *Kommunist*, the main party journal, condemned unidentified "enemies of the principles of peaceful coexistence" who failed to see that these principles were gaining increasing influence on international relations.[14] The presumption that this censure was directed at internal opposition was borne out when Andrei Gromyko, a Politburo member then serving as foreign minister, offered a justification of détente clearly directed at domestic critics. Asserting that "the future belongs to détente," Gromyko pointedly recalled Lenin's strictures against hotheaded Soviet radicals ready to abandon diplomacy for a risky course of confrontation with the West. Drawing an implicit parallel with Soviet efforts to derail the planned U.S. INF deployments by appealing to Western Europe, Gromyko emphasized the contemporary relevance of Lenin's diplomatic tactic of using some imperialist states to curb others. Strikingly, he praised the benefits of arms-control and other negotiations during the 1970s and completely omitted any mention of the deterioration of East-West relations during the early 1980s.[15]

Despite such ripostes, criticism of existing policy has continued. In September 1984, for example, the party chiefs were preparing to announce Marshal Ogarkov's demotion to a lesser position and were pondering whether to resume the superpower arms talks they had broken off a year earlier in protest against the beginning of the U.S. INF deployments. Their deliberations over these issues obviously provoked discord, because a member of the editorial board of *Kommunist* chose the moment to defend the workability of superpower détente in terms that were clearly more than pro forma. The editor castigated "realists" and "well-intentioned skeptics who, alluding to the sharply increased tension in the world, consider that the times of détente have supposedly receded into the past and that in the current situation it is, at the least, superficial and naive to think about any sort of future for détente."[16] Together with other evidence of high-level conflict over the renewal of arms negotiations, the description of these anti-détente skeptics as "well-intentioned" indicates that they were members of Soviet rather than Western ruling circles. The timing of such incidents demonstrates that on certain crucial policy questions a hard-line minority has lobbied vigorously for a more confrontational policy toward the United States.[17]

To date, more measured views have usually prevailed, and General Secretary Gorbachev seems firmly committed to improving Soviet-American relations by political means. Nevertheless, during the past five years the critique of established policy from Soviet conservatives has garnered enough internal support to put such leaders as Brezhnev and Chernenko on the political defensive,[18] and similar pressures are being exerted on Gorbachev. According to Anatoly Dobrynin, the new party secretary responsible for overseeing foreign policy, Gorbachev's heightened accent on venturesome diplomacy and "reasonable compromises" with the United States has been accompanied by "fierce collisions, sharp discussions, and painful disagreements" within the political elite.[19] As explained below, some of the disagreements have centered on how to cope with SDI.

The recurrence of such conflicts within the party leadership testifies to genuine soul-searching and apprehension about current U.S. political and military strategy toward the USSR. Soviet observers manifestly disagree about whether U.S. policy requires the rapid inauguration of new Soviet defense programs or whether it requires countermeasures over the longer term only. No doubt this is one reason why the Soviets have clashed over the operational meaning of the official slogan that the danger of war is increasing. Officials such as Gromyko wish to use this theme primarily as a diplomatic tool to influence Western opinion and forestall the long-term threat, whereas figures such as Ogarkov believe that foreign opinion is irrelevant to the imminent danger facing the USSR.

In a general sense, however, Soviet observers all agree that the United States has embarked on a major drive to overturn the international position attained by the USSR through more than two decades of painstaking effort, and they view the Strategic Defense Initiative as part of that campaign. In 1980, well before President Reagan was elected or announced SDI, Soviet observers began to express apprehension that the shifting U.S. outlook exemplified by the nonratification of the SALT II agreement might lead the United States to discard the ABM treaty, and after the Reagan administration took office defense officials began to warn of the danger of a wholesale U.S. abrogation of arms-control treaties.[20] Although these statements may have been meant purely as propaganda, this seems unlikely in view of the internal Soviet controversy over the utility of arms-control agreements as instruments for containing the U.S. military buildup. At any rate, the advent of SDI has given ample substance to such fears.

On the political level, SDI symbolizes a threat to the USSR's international standing as a superpower. From the Soviet standpoint, one of the principal achievements of the détente of the 1970s was that it won U.S. and third-party recognition of the USSR as the United States' geopolitical equal, and Soviet decisionmakers resent the fact that the United States has now apparently withdrawn that recognition. Compared with the diverse assortment of economic, political, and military resources available to the United States, Soviet decisionmakers must depend disproportionately on military instruments of policy, which makes strategic equality an especially important symbol of the USSR's superpower status. If the Americans create a radical new type of weaponry that the USSR does not possess, this will be a major political setback and will undermine the regime's image at home and abroad.[21]

At the same time, SDI constitutes a challenge to the technological dynamism of the Soviet system. For decades the Soviets have taken pride in the centrally planned economy that has enabled them, with fewer resources at their disposal, gradually to close the military gap separating the USSR from the other great powers. The Strategic Defense Initiative, however, raises serious questions about whether the Soviet economy will prove able to generate the new types of technology now being incorporated into Western military planning. SDI thus poses systemic demands that extend far beyond the military realm, and it has become entangled with the Soviet leadership's overall strategy of economic modernization and political change.

In the final analysis, of course, the urgency of the political and economic challenges stems from the potential military implications of SDI. As viewed from Moscow, the U.S. turn to space systems represents an extension of the drive for strategic superiority that almost all Soviet observers regard as a self-evident feature of recent U.S. policy. The novelty of SDI is that it exemplifies, more than any other U.S. military program, an emerging effort to outflank the USSR by shifting the arms competition to new realms of technology and devaluing Soviet strengths in current types of military hardware.[22] For Soviet strategists and force planners, this new pattern of weapons competition introduces a worrisome element of unpredictability into a military rivalry that the 1972 signing of the Anti-Ballistic Missile Treaty helped direct into narrower channels and make more manageable. When general secretary Iury Andropov replied to President Reagan's announcement of SDI in March 1983, he asserted that the program would undercut the basic understanding about the interaction between offensive and defensive weapons that the superpowers had reached in the SALT I negotiations.[23]

The strategic uncertainties introduced by SDI seem especially large to Soviet observers because they are convinced that SDI will be used to augment, rather than to supplant, other U.S. weapons programs. In responding to Reagan's announcement, Andropov depicted SDI as one of a series of threatening military trends. The United States, he claimed, was engaged in a rapid qualitative improvement of all its military forces, particularly its strategic offensive forces, which had grown during the previous twenty years from 4,000 to more than 10,000 nuclear weapons. Andropov also asserted that the United States was planning to deploy more than 12,000 long-range cruise missiles against the USSR.[24] Soviet military commentators have portrayed SDI as an integral part of a U.S. drive to attain superiority over the USSR by developing more accurate offensive nuclear weapons able to destroy hardened Soviet intercontinental ballistic missile (ICBM) silos as well as to devise highly sophisticated methods of electronic warfare and more lethal precision munitions for use in conventional conflicts.[25]

For this reason, virtually all Soviet commentators dismiss U.S. assurances that the purpose of a deployed SDI system would be strictly defensive. Andropov contended that SDI and the U.S. offensive buildup were complementary policies designed to give the United States a capacity to launch a disarming nuclear strike against the USSR with impunity.[26] Soviet suspicions are reinforced by the fact that in past discussions of a potential U.S. ballistic missile defense some U.S. BMD supporters advocated acquiring such a capability, even though they have seldom made this argument publicly since the president announced SDI.[27] In the Soviet view, SDI could serve a critical offensive function by encouraging the United States to launch a nuclear strike against the USSR on the assumption that the strike would destroy many Soviet ballistic missiles and that U.S. defenses could neutralize the surviving missiles fired in retaliation.

Partly for this reason, Soviet strategists find little consolation in the notion that the United States probably cannot devise a "leakproof" BMD system—that is, one that could intercept nearly all the missiles in a Soviet first strike.[28] Used offensively, a U.S. system would need to be less efficient than if it was purely defensive, since many Soviet missiles would (presumably) be destroyed in the initial U.S. attack and would never be fired. Possession of a less-than-perfect BMD system, Soviet analysts maintain, could still have a critical influence on U.S. decisionmakers pondering whether to use nuclear weapons against the USSR. Further, they contend that the existence of a U.S. BMD system would strengthen the U.S. inclination to try to fight a limited nuclear war in Europe on the assumption that the American homeland could be protected against Soviet nuclear strikes.[29]

Consistent with their skepticism that SDI is intended to serve a purely defensive purpose, the Soviets claim that a U.S. space-based BMD system will ultimately be designed to strike not only Soviet missiles in flight but Soviet terrestrial targets. In 1983 Ustinov stated that a U.S. refusal to conclude an agreement banning the deployment of "space strike weapons" would signify a U.S. intention to deploy space weapons "capable of aiming not only at targets in space, but also at our entire planet."[30] More specifically, other commentators have charged that space-based systems could be used "for destroying the armed forces in their starting positions, the command and control complex, the economy, the infrastructure, and the population of the other side."[31] Gorbachev has also raised this possibility.[32] Some Soviet specialists have implied that this development could occur only in the long run, well after the United States acquires the capacity to use space-based defenses in conjunction with offensive ballistic missiles to neutralize Soviet strategic forces, but they have still insisted that it is a real possibility.[33] In other words, space-based systems might become direct, rather than indirect, instruments of a U.S. first strike against the USSR—one that could be launched almost instantaneously, without the ten to thirty minutes' warning currently afforded by submarine-launched ballistic missile (SLBM) and ICBM trajectories.

Whether such attacks from space against terrestrial targets will ever become technically feasible remains highly uncertain. At present many Western experts qualified to judge this issue evidently believe they will not, although a few think that instantaneous attacks from space, particularly on unhardened targets, might eventually be possible.[34] Faced with such uncertainties, however, Soviet officials must make working assumptions about the likely strategic environment of the future. Even if the more skeptical assessment of launching direct terrestrial strikes from space is ultimately borne out, Soviet perceptions of SDI's implications depend less on current tests of technical feasibility than on worst-case scenarios of coming possibilities. America's history of outstanding technological achievements, together with the Soviets' natural wariness about so vital a security issue, predispose Soviet strategists to believe that if weapons are stationed in space, sudden enemy strikes from space will sooner or later become possible.[35]

For all these reasons, Soviet policymakers contend that a competition in building and deploying large BMD systems will mark a watershed in Soviet-American relations. Although all recent general secretaries have sounded this warning, Gorbachev has spelled out his view of the potential consequences with particular force. He has warned that the introduction of weapons into space would "signify a qualitatively new jump in the arms race which would inevitably lead to the disappearance of the very concept of strategic stability—the foundation of the preservation of peace in the nuclear century." The deployment of space-based BMD systems, he has claimed, will create a situation in which fundamental and possibly irreversible strategic decisions "would be taken essentially by electronic machines, without the participation of human reason and political will.... Such a development of events could lead to a universal catastrophy," including a catastrophy caused by human miscalculation or technical malfunction. Deployment "could transform the current strategic balance into strategic chaos," prompting an unregulated arms race, increasing distrust among states, and diminishing their security.[36]

In appraising such statements, Western observers are entitled to a measure of skepticism, since the Soviets have regularly voiced concern about most major U.S. weapons and have tried to influence U.S. arms decisions by political means. They have, for example, complained repeatedly that the MX and Pershing II missiles are instruments of aggression intended to give the United States a capacity to launch an incapacitating first strike against the USSR.[37] Nonetheless, Soviet complaints and warnings about other weapons have never been as sweeping and categorical as those about SDI, nor have other weapons been discussed as voluminously by the Soviet media. Perhaps the best illustration of the special treatment given SDI can be found in Andropov's speeches. In 1983, at the peak of the Soviet diplomatic campaign to block the deployment of U.S. missiles in Europe, Andropov said that installation of the missiles would be "a major move fundamentally inimical to peace." In contrast, he called SDI a "mine" planted beneath the whole arms-control process and classed it as a program that could "radically upset the concept of strategic stability and the very possibility" of effective arms limitations.[38]

It is improbable that these unusually stark statements about the implications of SDI are simply public posturing designed to serve Soviet negotiating tactics. This explanation not only fails to explain the absence of equivalent Soviet pronouncements about other prospective U.S. weapons; it also fails to consider the negative political impact of such statements on the Soviet bargaining position. Expressions of apprehension, it is true, may elicit sympathetic responses from Western groups already opposed to SDI. But they may also encourage the Reagan administration's more assertive members to press forward with SDI and the more moderate members to demand radical Soviet military concessions in exchange for limiting it. Gorbachev himself has recently recognized and tried to reduce this political liability.[39] On balance, therefore, the force of the pronouncements suggests that Soviet policymakers do indeed view SDI as the potential harbinger of a new era of unstable strategic relations with the United States and that they regard that prospect with genuine alarm.

# 3.
# SOVIET POLICY TOWARD
# SOVIET BMD AND THE
# MILITARY USES OF SPACE

The USSR's policies toward the use of BMD and space-based weapons for its own defense have been shaped by long-standing strategic goals. Historically, although the USSR has sometimes invaded countries much weaker than itself, it has almost always been extremely cautious about risking wars with other great powers that might endanger the Soviet system. In keeping with this aim, the regime has striven to build and maintain a powerful military establishment capable of deterring enemy attack and defeating any state that launches a war against the USSR. A further goal, grounded in vivid memories of the massive destruction wrought by the Nazi invasion, has been to minimize war damage to Soviet society by building not only strong offensive forces but also strong strategic defenses. Finally, in the past two decades the regime has sought to avoid engaging potential enemies in arms races that have a large prospect of worsening the USSR's military position relative to those opponents.[1]

At the practical level, however, such strategic goals are often incompatible with one another, and policymakers must decide which to give primacy.[2] They must, for instance, weigh a desire for forces capable of protecting their homeland and defeating the enemy against a desire to avoid forms of arms competition that may put them at a military disadvantage. Choices of this kind require decisionmakers to make broad judgments about the intentions and capabilities of their country's potential enemies, about the possible range of conflict or cooperation in international politics, and about the dynamics of modern military technology.[3] The Soviet analysts and officials concerned with BMD have sometimes disagreed about these matters, and the prevailing Soviet attitude toward BMD has changed over time.

As late as the mid-1960s Soviet proponents of BMD were inclined to treat the mutual nuclear vulnerability of the superpowers as a destabilizing factor that would engender international crises. As one influential Soviet strategic thinker, retired Major General Nikolai Talensky, put it, the combination of strong offensive forces and an effective ABM system would "substantially increase the stability of mutual deterrence." By contrast, adopting a policy of deterrence through mutual vulnerability would leave the Soviet Union in the unacceptable position of gambling its security "on the goodwill of the other side."[4] It need hardly be said that the theory of mutual assured destruction (sometimes referred to as MAD) rests on each side's rational calculation of its own self-interest rather than its goodwill toward the other. But Soviet theorists were unwilling to assume that a rational self-interest would reliably prevent the Western nuclear powers from launching a nuclear attack against the USSR. An occasional Soviet commentator may have voiced doubt about the feasibility of creating an effective BMD system and observed that the doctrine of deterrence posited by the theory of mutual assured destruction has "a definite logic." But even commentators such as these acknowledged that MAD neglects the vital problems of accidental war and war through Western miscalculation.[5]

In this period the dominant Soviet view corresponded to the position laid down in 1967 by *Pravda*. In February prime minister Kosygin, when queried by a foreign correspondent about the possibility of concluding a treaty to limit ABM systems, declined to answer directly. According to the *Pravda* account, however, he asked rhetorically whether it was defensive or offensive systems that raise international tensions, clearly implying that it was the latter. According to the report, Kosygin drew a sharp distinction between the functions of offensive and defensive weapons. Making no reference to the possibility that possession of an ABM system might encourage an aggressor to launch a surprise attack, he reportedly observed that even though an ABM system might cost more than offensive weapons, it "prevents attack" and is intended "not to kill people, but to save human lives."[6] The fact that the version of the press conference printed by *Pravda* was a seriously inaccurate rendering of Kosygin's tape-recorded remarks suggests that by 1967 the Soviet leadership debate over the wisdom of entering Soviet-American talks on strategic arms had become intertwined with internal disagreements over the desirability of deploying a system of ballistic missile defense.[7] But publication of the emended text also shows that the prevailing view continued to be that BMD was not conducive to strategic instability and crises.

   *Pravda*'s account reflected the assumptions that guided the construction of the Soviet air defense network in the years following World War II. During the 1950s the USSR developed and deployed an extensive system of interceptor aircraft and surface-to-air missiles (SAMs) intended to counter enemy bombers; within a decade this system had grown to encompass about 3,700 aircraft and 1,000 SAM sites.[8] In the mid-1950s the government also began to develop its first BMD components. In the early 1960s it started to build a ring of defensive missiles intended, perhaps, to protect the city of Leningrad against enemy ballistic missiles, and within a few more years began building a different system definitely meant to provide antimissile defense for the Moscow region. Technically unsophisticated and extremely costly, these early systems represented an instinctive tendency to put a premium on strategic defense and to pursue it with respect to enemy ballistic missiles as well as enemy aircraft.[9]

   In addition to denying any connection between BMD and crisis instability, Soviet officials during these years discounted the idea that the development of BMD systems would contribute significantly to the arms race. In the 1967 interview, for instance, *Pravda* quoted Kosygin to the effect that ABM weaponry was "not a cause" of the arms race but a factor that prevents the death of people.[10] Here, too, Kosygin's remarks were not accurately rendered by the newspaper, but the printed version clearly implied that ABM systems would not contribute to an action-reaction cycle between defensive and offensive weapons.[11]

   In the first half of the 1960s most of the Soviet commentators who discussed the feasibility of building an effective ABM system were technological optimists. During this period, although occasional dissenting voices asserted that the triumph of the offense over the defense was "final" and that an effective defense against nuclear weapons "cannot be created," senior political leaders, Ministry of Defense officials, and military writers repeatedly expressed optimism that effective ABM systems could indeed be devised.[12] Just as important, Soviet commentators appeared confident that the Soviet Union was better equipped to build such a system than was the United States. No doubt this attitude resulted partially from the buoyant technological optimism of the Khrushchev era, when *Sputnik* and other Soviet technological feats prompted the ebullient party leader to predict that the Soviet Union would surpass the United States in per capita output within a decade.[13]

In a period when Soviet socialism seemed technologically more dynamic than American capitalism, the question of whether the progress of military weaponry could be controlled by diplomatic means was not especially pressing. For the Soviets who bothered to consider the issue, however, there were few encouraging precedents for negotiated limitations on the superpower arms competition. Multilateral negotiations to ban nuclear weapons were being held under the auspices of the United Nations, and the Limited Test Ban Treaty confining nuclear weapons tests to underground explosions had been signed in 1963. But no Soviet-American agreement limiting actual weapon deployments had yet been achieved. The two superpowers were just beginning to move toward other agreements, such as the 1967 treaty banning weapons of mass destruction in outer space and the 1968 nuclear nonproliferation treaty, which provided some encouragement for Soviet officials who believed that negotiations might yield useful curbs on the deployment of weapons.[14]

By the final third of the 1960s Soviet judgments about BMD's impact on superpower relations during crises began to change markedly. As the large Soviet military buildup brought the USSR closer to strategic parity and improved its technical ability to detect surprise attacks, Soviet decisionmakers became more confident that the threat of certain retaliation would deter U.S. nuclear strikes. This new confidence, in turn, encouraged them to downgrade the value of BMD and accept that it might undermine crisis stability.[15] Publicly, Soviet commentators hesitated to endorse the theory of mutual assured destruction because the theory entailed an ideologically unpalatable acknowledgment that the "peace loving" USSR might need to be deterred and because the idea that nuclear vulnerability might confer any strategic benefit was deeply distasteful to a country that had suffered extraordinary damage during World War II. Nevertheless, Soviet officials did repeatedly acknowledge in public the existence of mutual strategic vulnerability between the superpowers,[16] and privately some spokesmen went further. In confidential diplomatic exchanges at the beginning of the Strategic Arms Limitations Talks (SALT) in 1969, the chief of the Soviet delegation stated that ABM systems, if deployed, might be destabilizing because they would create uncertainty in the mind of a potential attacker about the ability of the potential victim to mount a devastating retaliatory strike.[17] The Soviet posture toward Soviet-American strategic arms negotiations, which regularly has sought to define the terms of any prospective talks or agreements so as to include ABM weapons, is consistent with the idea that such statements were more than mere rhetoric. Further, as the 1970s progressed, these views gradually filtered into the public domain. In 1979, several years after the ratification of the SALT I agreements and shortly after the signing of the SALT II accord, another Soviet commentator stated that the "balance of fear" created by each side's retaliatory capability is "the best guarantee of security" for the superpowers.[18]

Soviet views on the connection between BMD systems and the arms race also shifted. In the 1970s a number of Soviet writers endorsed the thesis that negotiated limitations on defensive weapons slow the superpower weapons competition. In 1972, for example, immediately after the conclusion of the SALT I treaties limiting both offensive strategic weapons and ABM systems, two of the Soviet SALT negotiators stressed that "strategic offensive and defensive armaments are closely connected with one another. The development of one of these forms of armament inevitably entails the development of the other, and vice versa—the arms race is continually being driven forward by this process. Therefore, in order reliably to block the way to a further buildup of arms, a decision is needed which would limit both strategic offensive armaments and systems for defense against their attack." The authors went on to cite with approval the view that in the absence of large BMD systems there would be no stimulus for either side to develop more powerful offensive systems.[19] They thereby took an intellectual step that seemed small but was actually very large, since it excluded the possibility that the principal cause of the superpower arms competition could be the contest for relative advantage between the offensive weapons of each side.

Most Soviet observers refrained from endorsing such a categorical view of the action-reaction cycle but did suggest that a limit on ABM systems would have a moderating effect on the pace of weapons innovation. During the Soviet legislative sessions convoked to ratify the SALT I agreements, deputy foreign minister Kuznetsov and Politburo member N.V. Podgornyi stated that the limits on BMD systems would slow the race in offensive arms.[20] Moreover, two leading professional officers also endorsed the idea that the ABM treaty could contribute to arms race stability. Marshal Kulikov, then chief of the General Staff, noted that the treaty would help prevent "the emergence of a chain reaction of competition between offensive and defensive arms."[21] Minister of defense Grechko similarly remarked that the treaty would "impede the development of the competition beween offensive and defensive nuclear missile arms."

Grechko, however, also emphasized that the treaty "does not impose any limits whatsoever on research and experimental projects directed toward solving the problem of defending the country from nuclear rocket strikes." Like the officers in charge of air defense, he wished to maintain the Soviet program of ABM research and clearly believed that the problem of defense against enemy ballistic missiles should ultimately be solved.[22] Exemplifying the outlook of the Soviet military SALT delegates who initially resisted the limit on "exotic" ABM technologies that was finally written into the ABM treaty,[23] Grechko's statement foreshadowed a later internal struggle over the pace and scope of Soviet ABM research.

The post-1967 appraisal of the role of ABM weaponry in the arms race was linked to alterations in Soviet perspectives on the chances of building an effective system, as well as to a new view of the U.S. potential to build such a system. In the mid-1960s a debate over the feasibility of building an effective BMD system flared up in the pages of *Military Thought*, the confidential journal of the General Staff. In this debate spokesmen for the National Air Defense Forces pushed for the construction of a large ABM system.

One leading air defense theorist, for example, argued that "in connection with the intentions of U.S. imperialists to harness space forces to the chariot of war, the necessity has arisen of keeping under control not only air space, but also cosmic space." As a result, the missions of the National Air Defense Forces "today have gone beyond the limits of combating offensive enemy aircraft. They must also be able to intercept and destroy ballistic missiles and space means of attack. In other words, a modern air defense must be anti-aircraft, antimissile, and anti-space."[24] As the debate bubbled up to the top levels of the Soviet government, the head of the National Air Defense Forces vigorously affirmed the feasibility of ABM defense and sought to present the broad definition of his service's mission as official party policy.[25]

By contrast, other officers voiced doubt about the feasibility of a Soviet ABM system and advocated countering U.S. strategic power through a further expansion of Soviet offensive forces. The commander of the Strategic Rocket Forces claimed that a salvo of ballistic missiles was invulnerable to countermeasures.[26] Arguing the case in detail, Lieutenant Colonel of Engineering V. Aleksandrov provided an analysis of U.S. ABM programs, which clearly implied that despite ongoing R and D efforts, an effective ABM system probably could not be built for some time. "Why," he asked, "hasn't the U.S., despite rather extensive scientific research and experimental design work in the field of antimissile defense, settled on some kind of definite plan for a system and begun actual construction of it?" The reasons, answered Aleksandrov, included "the imperfection and insufficient effectiveness of the systems which have been studied" and "the extremely high cost of deployment and the relatively small political advantages over the enemy which would be achieved by the very costly wide or even partial deployment of a system of limited effectiveness." The most substantial result of U.S. work on ABM systems, he claimed, had been to reveal more effective ways of overwhelming antimissile defenses. "In every phase of this work it has been shown that the development and perfection of offensive means are more promising, cheaper, and simpler." Without disagreeing, Aleksandrov cited the view of a leading U.S. defense official that "there theoretically is no antimissile defense which cannot be overcome by an enemy. The more effective an antimissile defense system, the greater the expenditures which will be required to overcome it. However, these expenditures do not compare with the cost of deploying the defensive system. And this is the most important advantage of means of penetrating the antimissile defense: They can be extremely effective with relatively small expenditures."[27] One striking feature of Aleksandrov's discussion was the use of American criticisms of BMD to counter Soviet BMD proponents.

Arguments like Aleksandrov's provoked rebuttals from the advocates of ABM weapons, who contended that Soviet nuclear forces could not defend the USSR against U.S. missiles and that only a Soviet ABM system could perform this function. For instance, Major General I. Zav'ialov criticized the Soviet theorists who believed that strategic defense had no role in a nuclear war. Zav'ialov acknowledged that Soviet strategic offensive forces had "a special place" in frustrating a Western nuclear attack. "But," he continued, "nuclear strikes at the enemy's means of nuclear attack can scarcely achieve their complete destruction. These means are dispersed over great land and water areas, are well protected under ground and under water, and a part of them under any circumstances will go into action. So the destruction of them in flight will be a basic element in modern strategic defense. In other words, strategic defense in a nuclear war is primarily air defense (antimissile, antiaircraft, and antispace), to be carried out over the territory of the whole country." According to this view, the difficulty of destroying enemy ballistic missiles through preemptive attack meant that Soviet ABM systems had a vital role to play in achieving a favorable correlation of strategic forces during wartime.[28]

This internal debate was linked to the Soviet decision to halt construction of some of the BMD installations being built around Moscow. Work on the Moscow BMD system, which was at first planned to include eight complexes with a total of 128 interceptor missiles, speeded up in 1966. The following year, however, construction continued on only six of the eight complexes. In 1968 work on two of the six was discontinued, and only four were finally completed.[29] This failure to follow through with the full deployment plans for the Moscow system indicates that the doubts voiced by some domestic critics had a tangible effect on Soviet BMD policy.

By the end of the decade public Soviet claims for the feasibility of developing a workable ABM system became much less common, and most Soviet military spokesmen began to describe the mission of the National Air Defense Forces, which had earlier been broadly construed to include defense against enemy ballistic missiles, as defense against enemy aircraft only. Senior air defense commanders resisted this narrowing of their service mission, but they were gradually compelled to pay lip service to the new formula.[30] Indicative of the shuffling of service priorities, some military theorists who had earlier championed BMD now began to accept the view that preemptive offensive strikes against enemy forces offered the only possible hope of limiting the damage Western missiles might inflict on the Soviet homeland.[31]

The shift in BMD policy was also influenced by a broad economic reappraisal that questioned the Soviet system's capacities for technological innovation and carried worrisome military implications. During the late 1960s some Soviet economists reached the unorthodox conclusion that the USSR was less technologically dynamic than the West, and their views filtered into the outlook of foreign-policy specialists and some Politburo members. The domestic controversy over Soviet technological performance vis-à-vis the West coincided with a debate over the desirability of beginning talks to limit offensive and defensive strategic arms, and the two issues were closely linked. In these internal deliberations, the proponents of arms talks were usually pessimistic about the Soviet technological future, whereas the opponents of negotiation remained optimistic about the USSR's prospects of surpassing the West technologically.[32] The pessimistic view of Western technological capabilities was not the sole cause of the Soviet decision to begin strategic arms negotiations, but it was a large contributing factor.

Another major contributing factor was the judgment that it was possible for the United States and USSR to cooperate to slow the development of military technology. This entailed a belief, first, that the West might be willing to negotiate such limitations and, second, that the structure of the international political system and the arms race would not necessarily nullify Soviet-American diplomatic efforts toward this end. At the time the SALT negotiations began some Soviet military spokesmen explicitly questioned these assumptions, but their reservations were rebuffed by foreign minister Gromyko, who condemned the suggestions of "good-for-nothing theorists" that "disarmament is an illusion."[33] In this period Soviet political leaders, after a period of highly negative depictions of the U.S. political elite, began to acknowledge the existence of Western officials and influential social groups genuinely interested in slowing the arms race.[34]

Thus, on each of the central issues affecting policy toward BMD, a dramatic change occurred in Soviet views during the late 1960s and early 1970s. It would be incorrect, however, to assume that this shift produced a full consensus within the elite. Not only did minister of defense Grechko voice reservations at the time the ABM treaty was signed; four years later, elements within the armed forces raised a much more open challenge to the military policies that the political leadership had accepted along with the ABM treaty. Although this challenge apparently had several causes, one major factor was the party leadership's decision around 1974 to slow the growth of the Soviet military budget. Whether or not the new policy was meant to apply to military R and D as well as other budgetary inputs is uncertain, but it clearly met resistance from Grechko, who warned against slackening the pace of military expansion and weapons innovation.[35] The spending slowdown crystallized philosophical differences that probably had existed in the elite during the early 1970s but that had been softened by the defense budget's continued rapid growth during the first half of the decade.

A key document in this internal challenge over BMD was a book written by the military theorist V.M. Bondarenko and published in mid-1976 by the Ministry of Defense. The book was sent to the printer scarcely two months after Brezhnev, at the 25th Party Congress, had glowingly described a dramatic improvement in the country's international situation and showed a clear inclination to upgrade the priority of consumer goods production vis-à-vis the military establishment and heavy industry.[36] By contrast, Bondarenko's book warned of the persisting political influence of "reactionary" Western circles and asserted repeatedly that détente had not become an irreversible process. Bondarenko stressed that in contemporary circumstances new weapons could appear suddenly and lead to "a rapid achievement of military-technical superiority." This circumstance, he said, made the active use of the latest findings of science for military purposes "an extremely acute requirement."[37] Vigorously criticizing another Soviet writer for endorsing the idea of a weapon so terrible that it would never be used, Bondarenko argued that such views exaggerated the deterrent effect of nuclear weapons on "imperialist" military calculations. Even though the imperialists faced sure destruction through retaliation, their irrational hatred of socialism might still cause them to attack, he claimed.[38] Plainly Bondarenko did not share the prevailing Soviet assumption that the West had a rational self-interest in survival and that the continuing vulnerability of the superpowers contributed to the military stability of their relationship.

Nor did Bondarenko accept the party's dominant assumptions concerning the dynamics of military technology and the possibility of controlling technology by political means. In an obvious allusion to offensive nuclear arms he derided the concept of an absolute weapon that could never be countered by defensive weapons. The belief in the insurmountable advantages of offensive systems, he said, ignored the dialectic between offensive and defensive weaponry. Thanks to this belief, he complained, "the impression is created that potential enemies must wait until the opposing side creates a weapon for their full annihilation, without taking any steps toward the creation of a similar weapon or toward the creation of effective means of defense against it."[39] But "such a thing has never happened in history. Experience teaches that the newest weaponry appears simultaneously in several countries. If potential enemies possess weaponry for a mutual strike, then the side which first creates the means of defense against it receives a decisive advantage. The history of the development of military technology is full of examples in which a weapon that had seemed irresistible and intimidating after a certain time was opposed by sufficiently reliable means of defense."[40]

Because the Russian word for "intimidation" is sometimes used as the equivalent of the English "deterrence," Bondarenko's phraseology implied that deterrence could easily be abrogated by the emergence of new defensive technologies. Elsewhere in the book he forcefully appealed for the acceleration of Soviet military research programs, and there can be no doubt that BMD research was high among his priorities.[41] The fact that he found it necessary to parry unnamed Soviet critics who claimed that the military R and D effort was hampering civilian development may mean that some officials were trying to slow the growth of military R and D, possibly including research on BMD.[42] At any rate, in view of the limits imposed by the ABM treaty on the development and deployment of BMD systems, it is significant that he seemed eager to protect the prerogatives of military researchers against curbs created by diplomatic agreements.[43]

Partly because it provoked interservice rivalries over service missions and budgets, the proposal to work toward an extensive Soviet BMD system apparently engendered resistance as well as support within the military establishment. Air defense reviewers of Bondarenko's book were unqualifiedly enthusiastic, but officers from other military branches expressed reservations that were strengthened by the proposal's infringement on their own institutional missions.[44] From a budgetary standpoint, the proposal impinged potentially on the interests of all the services. From a functional standpoint, however, it had special implications for the Strategic Rocket Forces (SRF), the branch that has customarily borne the main responsibility for deterring a Western nuclear attack and for weakening such an attack through preemptive strikes if it appears inevitable.

In a book published at the same time as Bondarenko's, air defense spokesmen argued vigorously for an expanded BMD system and implicitly denigrated the role of the SRF. Asserting that the United States was still seeking nuclear superiority over the USSR, these spokesmen warned that the threat of a U.S. surprise attack remained "entirely real" and that any nuclear counterforce exchange would inevitably entail massive collateral damage to the populations and economies of the warring states.[45] The writers acknowledged the great technical difficulty of defending against enemy ballistic missiles, but they also approvingly cited the opinion of "foreign specialists" that "strategic offensive forces are able merely to weaken the strikes of the air-space enemy.... [T]he defense of the economy and population of the country from the air, the ensuring of the normal life of the state, and the preservation of the fighting ability of its armed forces must fall to the means of antiair defense."[46] Along with other elements of their analysis, this statement implied that in case of nuclear war Soviet counterforce strikes would be insufficient to protect the USSR from devastation or to ensure military success,[47] and it supported their claim that "it is necessary to create...means" of defense capable of destroying incoming ballistic missiles.[48] Urging that the air defense system be continuously upgraded and able to destroy not only air-breathing weapons but also ballistic missiles and satellites, the authors remarked that "now victory or defeat in war has become dependent on how much the state is in a position to reliably defend the important objects on its territory from the destruction of strikes from air or space."[49]

The writers justified this attempt to expand the mission of the National Air Defense Forces partly by highlighting the U.S. decision to equip U.S. missiles with multiple independently targeted warheads (MIRVs) and thereby triple the number of U.S. strategic nuclear warheads.[50] Precisely how much of their concern was due to this authentic increase in the U.S. strategic threat, and how much to the fiscal threat hanging over their service budget, is unclear. At any rate, the book linked the task of countering enemy ballistic missiles to "the continuous process of rearmament and assimilating new battle technology," and it contained a foreword in which Marshal P. F. Batitskii, commander of the National Air Defense Forces, commended it to readers "interested in the development of antiair defense."[51]

Probably under political pressure, this open doctrinal challenge was quickly muted. Accepting a narrower definition of his service's mission, Batitskii soon published a pamphlet that focused exclusively on the threat posed by Western air-breathing weapons and studiously ignored any mention of Western ballistic missiles or the need to counter them.[52] Apparently, however, this about-face came too late. By 1978 Batitskii had been demoted from his post and the budget of the National Air Defense Forces had begun to shrink in absolute terms, along with the budget of the Strategic Rocket Forces.[53]

The doctrinal challenge over BMD thus failed to affect basic Soviet policy toward strategic defense, although it may have exerted a narrower influence on policy toward R and D on ASAT and BMD weapons. In the year when the challenge occurred, the Soviets resumed the testing of a primitive ASAT system. Work on this system, which the USSR had originally developed in the wake of the United States' acquisition of rudimentary ASAT weapons, had been suspended at the end of 1971.[54] The available evidence suggests that the Soviet resumption of testing in 1976 was the result of an autonomous decision rather than a response to U.S. interest in ASAT weaponry or a "bargaining chip" against the possibility of ASAT talks.[55] Nevertheless, ASAT weapons evidently still ranked as a low Soviet priority, and in 1978, when the Soviets entered negotiations with the United States to ban such weapons, they again suspended tests of the system.[56] The 1978 suspension showed that the Soviet government was not committed to a rapid upgrading of the largely ineffectual system it had already created or to the rapid development of a more effective alternative that would utilize sophisticated infrared sensors to home in on targets.[57] In early 1980, after the United States responded to the invasion of Afghanistan by declining to continue the talks, the Soviet Union again began ASAT tests and was subsequently reported to be developing a larger booster to enable its system to attack satellites in geosynchronous orbits. However, as part of a new bid for ASAT talks, the government once more suspended tests in June 1982 and declared a testing moratorium that still remained in effect in the autumn of 1986.[58]

In the late 1970s and early 1980s the Soviets undertook a significant modernization of the Moscow BMD system and pursued an active program of BMD research and development. Although the USSR refrained from raising the number of ABM interceptors in the Moscow ABM system to the ceiling permitted by the ABM treaty, it did develop new transportable phased-array radars and new types of interceptor missiles technically superior to those already deployed around Moscow.[59] In the late 1970s it also began a program intended to upgrade the Moscow ABM system by replacing Galosh launchers with the new interceptors and improving the system's radar capacities.[60] Apparently this program, which falls within the activities permitted under the treaty and probably was motivated by an interest in improved protection against attacks from minor nuclear powers, represents the fruits of conventional R and D programs that have existed for some time. In addition, during the early 1980s the regime began developing an antitactical ballistic missile (ATBM). This type of weapon, which is not prohibited by the treaty and is intended for use against short-range ballistic missiles, is also likely, when deployed, to have some defense capability against strategic ballistic missiles, particularly SLBMs.[61] Meanwhile the Kremlin has maintained an extensive R and D effort intended to reveal the feasibility of applying high-energy lasers and particle beams to ballistic missile defense. Although measuring the size of Soviet military R and D activities is exceptionally difficult, official U.S. estimates state that more than 10,000 scientists and engineers are involved in the laser program.[62]

On balance, however, the upgrading of the Moscow system has improved only marginally the Soviets' ability to defend their capital from the enormous number of U.S. missiles that could be fired at it. The improved system would have little utility against a massive U.S. strategic attack, although it could provide some protection against theater weapons like the Pershing II and against third-country attacks and accidental launches.[63] While Soviet development of an ATBM system is a matter for Western concern, by itself the weapon will not lead to a decisive increase in Soviet BMD capabilities.

The prospects for obtaining advantageous results from Soviet research into exotic BMD technologies also remain uncertain. Soviet work on potential applications of ground-based lasers for terminal defense reportedly faces serious technical obstacles, and Western intelligence analysts have estimated that the Soviets would be unable to create prototypes of space-based particle-beam weapons before the year 2000 or thereabouts.[64] The claims of some administration spokesmen that the Soviet research program on space-based BMD is ''the most advanced...on the face of the Earth'' are seriously misleading. Although abreast of the United States in directed energy research, the USSR lags in many complementary technologies that would be essential to transform directed-energy weapons into effective BMD systems. A study by the Department of Defense shows that the Soviet Union trails the United States in computers and software, radar, electro-optical sensors, guidance and navigation, microelectronics, robotics, signal processing, and telecommunications.[65]

Despite the doctrinal challenge in the mid-1970s and the large scale of Soviet R and D programs, at the start of the 1980s the balance of Soviet elite opinion toward BMD was little changed. It still assumed a situation of mutual vulnerability between the superpowers, and it continued to hold that the absence of BMD on both sides was a stabilizing factor in the superpower relationship. One influential Soviet commentator remarked, ''It is obvious that an equilibrium in the sphere of strategic possibilities works for peace, and not war. To live in a situation of the 'balance of terror' is not very comfortable, but nevertheless equilibrium is better for the stability of the situation than is its absence." The writer attacked SDI and clearly felt that the introduction of BMD systems would undermine the stability of the superpower relationship.[66] Most Soviet observers also claimed that the absence of BMD systems helped to curb the arms race. These arguments were made with special force after President Reagan announced SDI, but their presence in the internal debates of the 1970s makes it likely that they represented a genuine view, not simply one advanced for the purpose of persuading foreign audiences.

Perhaps the most vital question for Soviet decisionmakers was whether the creation of an effective BMD system was becoming technologically feasible. In the 1980s many Soviet politicians and observers reiterated their doubts on this point. In a book published before the unveiling of SDI, two Soviet specialists argued that while contemporary BMD had attained "a truly fantastic degree of perfection," it "nonetheless is not absolute and does not give a full guarantee of security" because even one warhead could kill an enormous number of people. In view of the possibility of using outer space for military purposes, they said, "One can assume that in the long run the historical conflict between weapons of attack and weapons of defense will evidently nonetheless tilt in favor of weapons of attack." In a world of nuclear ballistic missiles, the old conception of defense "loses its meaning," and the only possible damage limitation measures available to a country under attack would consist of an immediate counterattack with offensive weapons. The ineluctable growth of nuclear arsenals, continued the authors, "has led to their beginning, in a certain sense, to negate themselves," and the self-negation of war as a means of resolving political conflicts has become "an objective necessity."[67] The authors remarked that if new limits on nuclear arms could not be negotiated, more ground-based ABM installations might ultimately be built. But they stated that ground-based BMD systems would not change the strategic balance, and their comments on the military uses of space implied that space-based BMD would yield more powerful offensive weapons instead of reliable defenses.[68] Their analysis suggested, first, that effective strategic defenses were unlikely to be devised in the foreseeable future and, second, that the consequences of nuclear war would be so catastrophic that the USSR's Western rivals would be unlikely to initiate such a conflict.[69]

However, important military figures apparently disagreed with this view. In 1978 Marshal Ogarkov, hinting that he sympathized with the need for more vigorous BMD research, dismissed the idea that the spiral between offensive and defensive weapons could be halted. "The history of war convincingly demonstrates," Ogarkov remarked,

> that the appearance of new means of attack has always led to the creation of corresponding means of counteraction.... This applies fully also to nuclear-missile weapons, whose creation and rapid growth impelled military-scientific thought and practice actively to work out means and measures of countering them. In its turn, the appearance of means of defense against weapons of mass destruction gave a new impulse to the perfecting of nuclear-missile means of attack. All of this confirms the conclusion that the age-old struggle between means of attack and defense...is one of the causes of the development of the means of battle and...of the methods of conducting military actions.[70]

Ogarkov's statement did not amount to a call for the immediate development and deployment of an extensive Soviet BMD system. It was phrased in such a way that it could be taken to mean that offensive weapons—in the form of ballistic missiles equipped with MIRVs and penetration aids, for example—still enjoyed a decisive advantage over defensive systems. But it clearly suggested that in the long run Soviet policymakers could not assume that this advantage would be preserved.

By 1982 Soviet views of ballistic missile defense and the military uses of space were becoming entangled in the broader foreign-policy debate discussed in chapter 2. In 1982 Ogarkov repeated his statement about the offense-defense interaction with slightly stronger phrasing that underscored the inevitability of the offense-defense linkage and its implications not only for the conduct of battles but the conduct of war in general.[71] Moreover, there was a sharp contrast of overall tone between the 1978 article in which he originally sounded this theme and the 1982 pamphlet in which he repeated it. The 1982 pamphlet contained a dire warning about the immediate military threat posed by the United States and demanded a drastic increase in military R and D and procurement to match the menacing acceleration of weapons innovation that Ogarkov claimed to discern in the West.

As indicated earlier, Ogarkov's campaign was part of a broader dispute about whether to rely mainly on diplomacy or new weaponry to counter the U.S. buildup, and it threw a weakened Brezhnev onto the political defensive in the last year of his life.[72] In October 1982 Brezhnev, under intense political pressure from party conservatives and military officers, promised that the pace of military R and D would be accelerated but apparently refused to increase military procurement. A few months later, in March 1983, the Christian Democrats won the West German parliamentary elections. Their victory, which greatly increased the probability that Soviet diplomacy would fail in its effort to prevent the deployment of U.S. intermediate-range missiles in Europe, strengthened Ogarkov's case that only a drastic Soviet military buildup could protect Soviet security. Coming in the same month, the announcement of SDI coincided with other serious setbacks for Soviet foreign policy and a major push from Soviet conservatives for more active weapons innovation.

It is difficult to say how the announcement of SDI affected the thinking of the military officials who felt that a large Soviet BMD system might ultimately have to be built. Judging by his general outlook on international politics and the arms race, Ogarkov was in theory the senior military policymaker most likely to push for a decision to build such a system. In 1984, for instance, he warned stridently against the West's stepped-up development of sophisticated weapons based on "new physical principles" and asserted that Soviet counterprograms must immediately be launched. However, while much remains uncertain about the evolution of Ogarkov's military preferences, the available evidence suggests that he did not favor a commitment to build an extensive Soviet BMD system. Although he emphasized Western military threats based on exotic technologies, the armaments he highlighted were sophisticated conventional weapons systems designed to interdict and destroy Soviet ground forces long before they could reach the battlefront. In contrast, Ogarkov did not refer directly to SDI.[73] Moreover, when he published the 1985 pamphlet reiterating his dire warnings about the West, he mentioned the dialectic between offensive weapons and counterweapons but omitted his earlier observation that this dialectic applied to nuclear missiles.

The most plausible explanation for this change is that Ogarkov, although skeptical about the possibility of curbing SDI through negotiations, was more concerned about what he perceived as an imminent Western conventional military threat and chose to play down the issue of BMD because he wanted to channel scarce resources into the development and production of more sophisticated conventional arms.[74] Other evidence suggests that the Air Defense Forces, which in the early 1980s underwent a name change and a drastic reorganization that squeezed their resources, may have favored a major expansion of the Soviet BMD system. This opinion, however, was probably not shared by most senior officers and certainly not by the party leadership as a whole.[75]

Although the recent controversies over security policy have not produced a basic change in Soviet attitudes toward BMD, they may help explain one case in which the Soviet Union has manifestly failed to adhere to the terms of the ABM treaty. In central Siberia, several thousand miles from the Soviet Pacific coast, the Soviets have begun constructing a large phased-array radar (LPAR) that faces eastward and is located some five hundred miles from the southern border. This step constitutes an unambiguous violation of the ABM treaty's requirement that such radars be situated only on the periphery of each superpower's territory and oriented outward. This treaty provision was intended to allow each country to maintain and develop peripheral LPARs capable of providing an early warning of enemy attack but to block the construction of LPARs in locations where they could be used to guide ABM interceptors to engage incoming enemy missiles. In 1983, when the United States discovered that a new LPAR was being built at Abalakovo, near Krasnoyarsk, some administration officials noted the proximity of this site to Soviet ICBM fields and charged that the USSR was violating the ABM treaty with the intention of building an extensive BMD system. The official Soviet explanation that the radar was intended solely for space tracking—as is permitted under the ABM treaty—struck many Western specialists as disingenuous.

Although a shortage of information prevents any firm conclusions about how senior Soviet officials made the decision to build the radar,[76] there are at least two explanations. One alternative, which assumes that the Abalakovo site was selected or approved during the heyday of détente in the mid-1970s, is that Soviet policymakers believed that the United States could be persuaded to accept the decision quietly, perhaps by referring to changes in the U.S. early-warning system that they believed were possible violations of the ABM treaty.[77] Another alternative is that although design work on the radar was begun in the 1970s, final authorization to build it at Abalakovo was not given until 1980 or 1981. According to this interpretation, the worsening relationship with the United States had produced more militant sentiments within the Soviet elite, including doubts about U.S. intentions to comply with SALT II and other arms agreements, and had increased the Soviet inclination to push beyond some of the limits established in those accords.[78]

However the choice was made, the construction of the Abalakovo radar does not prove that the Soviet Union has decided to deploy an extensive BMD of its own. A detailed CIA appraisal of the technical features of the installation, which is still being built, suggests that the radar has the wrong characteristics to serve as an ABM engagement radar and provide battle management for such a system. Reportedly the radar will operate at a relatively low radio frequency that is inappropriate for ABM functions and that makes it more susceptible to "blackouts" from nuclear explosions during an enemy attack. In addition, the radar face points toward the horizon. One would expect this feature in an early-warning radar designed to detect enemy ballistic missiles rising over the horizon at great distances, but not in an ABM radar, which must track incoming enemy warheads descending at a steep angle through the atmosphere. Finally, unlike the multiple-face Moscow ABM radar permitted under the ABM treaty, the Abalakovo installation has but one receiving face, which will enable it to track only ballistic missiles launched from submarines in the northern Pacific, not ICBMs traveling over the North Pole.[79] If the Soviets intended the Abalakovo radar to play a significant role in a future large ABM system, they have made a series of strikingly bad technical choices.

Much more plausible is the explanation that the Soviet government decided to build the Abalakovo radar to fill a gap in its early-warning radar coverage.[80] The Soviets had already decided, probably in the early 1970s, to upgrade their early-warning radar network by building peripheral LPARs at Pechora and other sites. The peripheral radars in this network—both those begun before and after Abalakovo—"have been constructed in priority order to respond to the deployment of new U.S. nuclear forces."[81] During the late 1970s the deployment of new Trident submarines with long-range missiles in the northern Pacific created a pressing need to fill the single large gap remaining in the coverage of the Soviet early-warning network.[82] Although the optimal site for an additional early-warning network would have been on the east coast of the Soviet Union, adequate coverage from the coast probably would have required two rather than one of these extremely expensive radars at a time when economic stringencies were impinging on the military budget with new force. A location near the coast would also have posed forbidding construction problems, particularly the necessity to build the massive installation on permafrost, which might melt, thereby shifting the foundations and degrading the radar's performance. Moreover, although radars based on the east coast would have provided several more minutes' warning of an attack launched against Soviet population and industrial centers from the northern Pacific, the other LPARs in the early-warning network cannot provide such long warnings of this sort of attack via polar and Mediterranean approaches. The Abalakovo site provides as much warning of such an attack from the east as the other LPARs would furnish of an attack from other directions. Put differently, even though the radar is not located on the Soviet border, it is an integral part of a perimeter of early-warning radars centered on Moscow.

This interpretation of the Abalakovo radar is reinforced by other evidence that, despite the presence of minority views within the elite, the Soviet leadership as a whole still wishes to avoid a commitment to build a large BMD system. Even if we accept the doubtful proposition that Ogarkov privately championed such a step, the party leadership's decision to demote him hardly constitutes a vote of confidence in the idea. More to the point, the leadership is now far more pessimistic about Soviet technological capacities vis-à-vis the West than it was twenty years ago. In recent years Soviet foreign-affairs specialists have cautioned against underestimating Western scientific and technological dynamism, and the main party journal has censured individuals who fail to take account of the relevance of this point to Soviet foreign policy.[83] Gorbachev has presented a much franker and more worrisome picture of Soviet economic troubles than Brezhnev ever did, and his pronouncements show a deep respect for U.S. capacities to innovate in both civilian and military technologies. Finally, the party leaders face an acute shortage of material resources even in the absence of an expensive new BMD program, and this shortage is already generating serious domestic strains. As shown in the next chapter, the elite has compelling economic reasons to try to avoid an all-out competition against the United States in BMD and space weaponry.

# 4.
# THE RESOURCE ALLOCATION DEBATE AND SOVIET BMD DECISIONS

The party chiefs have resisted a commitment to develop and deploy an extensive BMD not only because they fear the military consequences of an all-out superpower competition in this realm, but because they fear the economic consequences. In recent years the central fact of the Soviet domestic scene—apart from the vagaries of succession politics—has been the further deterioration of the country's economic performance. Still growing, the economy is not in danger of collapse, as exaggerated Western reports have occasionally suggested. But it is growing slowly, and there is a real possibility that the rate of expansion may decline still more in the coming years. The gap between the Soviet and U.S. gross national products, after diminishing slightly in Brezhnev's first decade as general secretary, has begun to widen. Perhaps even more important, Soviet inability to sustain rapid advances in a number of crucial technologies has made the USSR's technological weaknesses increasingly evident. Like other Soviet economic problems, these deficiencies have sometimes been overdrawn in the West, but they are nevertheless very real, and they raise major new dilemmas for party and military policymakers. Because of the shortage of resources, Soviet economic strategists find themselves under mounting pressures that are already formidable even in the absence of an all-out race in BMD.[1]

To understand these pressures, we need to refer again to the budgetary decisions of the mid-1970s. Around 1974, after a decade of rapid Soviet military expansion, the Brezhnev leadership adjusted its spending priorities. The causes of this adjustment included a more positive appraisal of the Soviet security situation and possibly the need to deal with internal economic problems that were beginning to worsen. By comparison with the preceding ten years, the regime's new resource allocation formula entailed slower growth of both military spending and economic investment and a continuation of the relatively high growth rate of popular consumption.[2]

Since about 1980, however, the declining performance of the domestic economy and the sharp deterioration of superpower relations have undermined this formula for resource allocation. To a far greater extent than during the past two decades, Soviet economic planners now face fundamental conflicts among divergent needs to invest in future economic growth, to improve consumer welfare, and to spend more on military programs. The party leaders want to upgrade the dynamism of the economy, and it has become increasingly evident that this will require a massive increase of capital investment, particularly in industry. However, they also face extraordinarily heavy investment demands from the energy complex and from agriculture, an especially inefficient sector in which they have already sunk vast quantities of resources with disappointing results. Some officials have been tempted to siphon the resources for industrial modernization from the rural sector, but agriculture, as well as light industry, requires more resources, not less, to satisfy the needs of the consumer. One alternative is to divert resources from the military budget. But this idea is at odds with the impulse to increase military spending in response to the dramatic U.S. military buildup of the past eight years.

In the 1980s these hard economic choices have sparked serious debates within the Soviet political elite. Even before President Reagan announced the Strategic Defense Initiative, signs of controversy over the level of Soviet military spending appeared. Backed by a Politburo faction that probably included G.V. Romanov and V.V.Shcherbitskii, Marshal Ogarkov and other professional officers urged that military spending be sharply increased.[3] By contrast, Brezhnev and such top-level allies as Konstantin Chernenko resisted a drastic increase in military spending. Instead, prompted partly by fears of a Soviet domestic upheaval like that in Poland, they advocated high priority for the consumer sectors, particularly agriculture, and pressed the military establishment to make more efficient use of the resources already at its disposal.[4] Meanwhile, yet another group within the elite argued for a sharp rise of economic investment, especially in heavy industry.[5] Although much remains to be clarified about the internal political alignments over these issues, the debate manifestly involved a serious conflict over the relative standing of military spending and other expensive items, such as Brezhnev's Food Program.

The resistance of the dominant Politburo coalition to demands for a jump in military spending, in turn, provoked new objections from senior officers. Ogarkov's hard-hitting article of May 1984 warned that Western military programs were proceeding at a breakneck pace and that a failure to respond promptly would be "a serious error" which would undermine Soviet security.[6] Two weeks prior to the appearance of this article, Chernenko had explicitly rejected a Soviet proposal for a special public campaign to support a larger military effort and had instead focused attention on the needs of agriculture and consumer welfare. Shortly after the publication of Ogarkov's blast, Chernenko, although decrying the deterioration of superpower relations, refrained from mentioning any need to strengthen the armed forces and told a meeting of military servicemen that the Soviet regime was doing "everything" required to ensure peaceful relations with the West.[7] In the 1980s open clashes of this kind have provoked sharp tensions in Soviet civil-military relations, and they clearly contributed to the party leadership's decision to demote Ogarkov in the fall of 1984.[8]

The controversy over economic priorities and military spending has encompassed not only the standard forms of economic resources but also the orientation of the national R and D effort. Although Soviet military programs have long commanded a very large share of total R and D, in the past ten or fifteen years there have been recurring debates over whether that share should be increased or decreased. The publication of Bondarenko's book in 1976 was a transparent attempt to enlarge the military's share and rebut the charges of civilians who contended that the size of the military R and D effort was hampering Soviet economic development.[9] Such military counterarguments may have enjoyed some success, since CIA estimates show that in the second half of the 1970s the growth rate for Soviet military R and D expenditures far exceeded the rate for the overall military budget and may have outpaced the rate for Soviet R and D as a whole.

In any event, debates over R and D have intensified during the 1980s. In 1980–81 Brezhnev, calling for the negotiation of super-power restraints on the creation of "qualitatively new" types of weapons, demanded that Soviet military R and D programs make a greater contribution to civilian needs and instituted an administrative review that apparently tried to implement this injunction.[10] By contrast, Ogarkov and some other outspoken military men accented the need to accelerate military R and D, particularly work on novel weapons.[11] This was a point of contention between Brezhnev and his military critics, and near the end of 1982, when he met with the assembled high command to deliver a defensive justification of his foreign policy, Brezhnev acknowledged a need to accelerate military R and D programs, although not military production.[12] Nevertheless, members of the military establishment have continued to press for a further enlargement of the military share of the national R and D effort. Once again, Bondarenko has been a spokesman for this view.[13]

The running controversy over military claims on economic resources has been mirrored in a "theoretical" debate over the sources of Soviet international power. While the terms of debate are complex, most of the participants seem to lean toward one of three basic views. The first view, which is probably held by many professional officers, maintains that the military threat from the West has already risen dramatically and calls for a sharp rise in current Soviet military spending. A second position suggests that economic development is more critical than current military production because the West poses no heightened military threat at present but may well pose such a threat ten to fifteen years hence. Thus the vital thing is to build up the advanced industrial sectors that can later be used to match new Western weapons systems. A third position holds that the greatest threat facing the regime is the potential for domestic unrest. Consequently popular welfare should receive top priority in order to shore up the regime's internal support and increase its international appeal and influence.[14]

The object lesson of Ogarkov's demotion has made the champions of military spending more cautious but has not eliminated tensions over the size of the defense budget. Although Gorbachev has firmly committed himself to build up the high-technology sectors of industry, his extremely ambitious targets for the rapid growth of investments have intensified short-term demands on economic resources and have strengthened the temptation to divert inputs previously earmarked for current military spending.[15] In his public statements as general secretary, Gorbachev has shown no more inclination than his immediate predecessors to underwrite a drastic expansion of the defense effort. Rather, he has bluntly asserted that the USSR's historical fate and future international standing depend on accelerating the economy's growth and expanding its high-technology sectors.[16] At a meeting with senior officers in the summer of 1985 Gorbachev delivered an unpublished speech rumored to contain a call for stringent limits on military expenditures, and at about the same time he apparently instituted measures to channel resources from defense production to civilian enterprises.[17] In addition, the guidelines for the new five-year plan instructed the defense industries to produce more consumer durables and equipment for the consumer industries than previously.[18]

In response to these signals, some officers have begun pressing for a stronger commitment to military needs. During the 1986 discussion of the new draft party program, for instance, some military theoreticians urged that the draft's rather equivocal formulas about equipping and manning the armed forces be strengthened.[19] Although these requests were deflected and the formula was changed only marginally, military pressures for stepped-up defense spending persisted, forcing Gorbachev to reassure "many of our people" that the USSR is not falling behind the United States militarily.[20] One recent manifestation of this pressure was the publication of an article by Ogarkov reiterating his earlier call for a rapid buildup of Soviet weaponry.[21]

Such tensions shed important light on the connections between Gorbachev's economic strategy and the task of countering SDI. A number of Western analysts have suggested that Gorbachev's emphasis on strengthening the economy's high-technology sectors has won widespread military support because it offers a ready-made prescription for matching the United States in a long-term competition in BMD and other sophisticated weapons systems. According to this view, the regime will first upgrade such industries as electronics, instrument manufacturing, and machine tools and will then be in a position to refurbish its stock of military hardware. Struck by the apparent fit between the modernization campaign and the challenge of SDI, a few scholars have even suggested that Gorbachev secretly welcomes SDI as a means of forcing through the drastic domestic economic reform he apparently desires.[22]

In actuality, however, the creation of a space-based BMD and the promotion of general economic modernization are incompatible goals, and the Soviet response to SDI is not a simple by-product of Gorbachev's domestic political agenda. Although economic modernization is indispensable for faster Soviet progress in developing space-based defenses, a crash campaign to match U.S. advances in this field will complicate and quite possibly defeat the modernization effort. In the short run, SDI may pose a smaller threat to economic modernization than do other Western military challenges, such as NATO's doctrine of Air-Land Battle, which require quicker deployments of new Soviet weapons in response. However, Soviet decisionmakers must cope with SDI in addition to these other challenges, not instead of them, and the effort to satisfy the added national-security demands on the economy could easily lead to institutional retrenchment rather than to economic reform.[23] The party is plainly striving to invigorate several branches of scientific research, particularly research on computers and information processing, that would be necessary to compete with the United States in space-based BMD.[24] But even if the programs of basic research necessary for an expanded BMD program and for general economic modernization prove more or less compatible, the requirements of the two goals will diverge as the development and engineering of BMD components consume a mounting share of R and D resources. A race in space-based BMD would quickly increase the demands on the scarce scientific and technical resources (especially various types of computer personnel) that are essential for upgrading civilian machine building and revitalizing the economy as a whole.[25]

Moreover, in the longer run SDI poses a direct threat to economic modernization. Even if the regime develops satisfactory prototypes of the necessary BMD components, it will face an enormous drain on conventional economic resources when the time comes to manufacture and deploy the system. Most knowledgeable Western economists believe that the USSR lacks enough investment resources to fulfill Gorbachev's extremely ambitious targets for economic growth, and some analysts foresee an impending conflict between the need for extensive civilian investment and the need to begin renovating the defense industries at the end of the 1980s.[26] In view of the obstacles that have plagued past attempts to reform the Soviet economy and improve economic performance, it is virtually certain that this shortage of resources cannot be overcome in time to shoulder an exponential increase in BMD production and deployment costs in the 1990s. Since Gorbachev has a realistic prospect of remaining general secretary well into the next century, he has every incentive to avoid the tremendous pressures that a commitment to an extensive BMD would put on the political system and on him personally.

Scarcely less important than the costs of BMD to civilian programs are the costs to other military programs. As noted above, the Soviets perceive themselves to be involved in an accelerating competition with the West in a wide range of military technologies. In a period of constrained growth of military budgets, a substantial share of the R and D and economic resources allocated to BMD will have to be taken from the programs of the other military services. In the Soviet Union, as in the West, tight budgetary contraints exacerbate intramilitary doctrinal disagreements, which often pit one service against another.[27] Soviet observers are aware of the revolution in computer and microelectronic technology spreading through all parts of the Western armed forces,[28] and there are already signs of disagreement over the priority to be assigned to the missions of the various Soviet armed services. Underscoring the growing possibility of conventional war between the superpowers, some military theorists have pushed hard for steps to counter Western advances in precision-guided munitions and other conventional arms, whereas other military writers have stressed the increasing importance of nuclear missiles and highlighted ''a relative reduction of expenditures on several types of conventional weapons.''[29] Under these conditions the Air Defense Forces, backed perhaps by elements of the General Staff and eager to secure an ample share of the military budget, may champion the development and deployment of a large BMD system. But other services are likely to resist the idea. Even during the late 1960s, when the total Soviet military budget was expanding rapidly, the Soviet debate over BMD drew the strategic rocket troops and the air defense forces into an institutional rivalry over which service could better protect the USSR against nuclear attack, and officers from other military branches showed greater skepticism about the feasibility of an effective ABM system than did air defense spokesmen.[30] In the 1980s and 1990s new budgetary pressures will spur the other services to scrutinize the idea even more critically.

Interservice rivalries of this sort are likely to have a sizable impact on Soviet decisions about deploying a large BMD system. The further the U.S. SDI program proceeds, the more strongly Soviet proponents will argue that an equivalent Soviet system is vital for Soviet national security. Under these conditions, a significant role may be played by highly placed military men from other services who choose to argue that SDI does not pose a grave threat or that an equivalent Soviet system is not the best response. Some military observers have already expressed oblique differences over whether SDI or trends in INF and conventional forces constitute the most threatening Western military programs.[31] Hypothetically, one can imagine the first deputy minister of defense for the Warsaw Pact arguing that SDI is less important than the need to spend more to counter the changes in NATO's doctrines and weaponry; on the other hand, the first deputy for Strategic Rocket Forces might accept that SDI is a serious threat but argue that a rapid expansion of the Soviet offensive ballistic missile force is the best way to counter it. As the debate becomes more intense, the civilian opponents of a large Soviet BMD system will enjoy a substantial advantage if they have part of the military establishment on their side, since the assessments of military professionals usually carry special weight in debates about the country's security situation.

There are thus strong internal forces working against a Soviet decision to enter into an all-out race with the United States in BMD technology. This, in turn, will influence the ways in which the Soviets respond to the further evolution of the U.S. SDI program.

# 5.
# SOVIET RESPONSES TO THE
# STRATEGIC DEFENSE
# INITIATIVE

Since the United States will not deploy an enlarged BMD system for at least ten more years and the USSR is already experiencing serious resource strains, Moscow's preferred response is to counter SDI through energetic diplomacy meant to produce strengthened arms limitations. On the one hand, the Soviets are trying to use direct contacts and more flexible arms-control proposals to convince U.S. policymakers that SDI should be curtailed. On the other, they are also striving through public diplomacy to generate pressure on administration officials who resist this idea. The Soviets have already taken a number of steps in pursuit of this policy, and they will undoubtedly take more. Only if such political approaches fail will the party leadership turn to major new military deployments as the chief method of countering the U.S. strategic defense program.

The policy emphasizing negotiation and political maneuver, however, faces definite obstacles. Internal Soviet resistance to the policy is already evident and will probably limit the additional military concessions Gorbachev and like-minded officials can make in superpower arms talks. In combination with the likely schedule of U.S. field tests and deadlines posed by the Soviet military procurement cycle, conservative uneasiness will increase pressures for a shift from a predominantly political to a predominantly military response to SDI. As explained below, this transition is likely to occur in the late 1980s and early 1990s.

In March 1983, immediately after Reagan announced SDI, Andropov launched the anti-SDI campaign with a hard-hitting speech, and more concrete steps followed in a few months. In August the Soviet delegation to the United Nations tabled the draft of a multilateral treaty prohibiting the use of force in outer space and from space against the earth. More specifically, the draft ruled out the testing and deployment of space-based weapons capable of attacking targets in outer space, the atmosphere, or on earth. It also called for a ban on the testing and creation of new ASAT systems, as well as for the dismantling of existing ASAT systems, although it included no details addressing the thorny problem of how the proposal for dismantling could be verified.[1] In the same month the treaty was proposed, Iury Andropov announced a Soviet moratorium on the placement of Soviet ASAT weapons in space. Promising that the moratorium would be observed as long as the United States refrained from further tests of its own ASAT system, Andropov explained shortly afterward that this offer included a moratorium on Soviet ASAT tests.[2]

At first glance, the submission of the 1983 treaty to the UN may seem merely a diplomatic ploy, but it may have been more. Although undoubtedly occasioned by the announcement of SDI, the draft was not simply a political improvisation, since it embodied several features of a similar treaty that the USSR had submitted to the UN in August 1981, a few months after Brezhnev called at the 26th Party Congress for arms-control efforts to limit futuristic weapons.[3] The 1981 treaty prohibited the stationing of weapons in space but did not deal with air-launched or ground-based ASAT systems such as those the Soviets were then testing; the 1983 treaty widened the coverage to prohibit these weapons as well. If Soviet policymakers were serious about negotiating new limits on space weapons in 1981, the choice of a multilateral rather than a bilateral forum still was probably logical, since in the summer of that year the Reagan administration was preoccupied with expanding U.S. military programs and remained reluctant to commence talks on strategic or intermediate-range nuclear arms—a reluctance reflected in the U.S. refusal to participate in the UN negotiations over the 1981 draft.[4] By proposing multilateral rather than bilateral negotiations on the 1983 draft treaty, the Soviets undoubtedly hoped to reap political gains in the diplomatic arena. But Soviet policymakers were probably also hesitant to bid for new bilateral arms talks when the United States was obviously intent on winning the political struggle to implement NATO's INF decision and when the Soviets themselves were hinting that they might break off existing negotiations if the INF deployments were carried out.

In any event, near the end of June 1984 Chernenko proposed direct talks between the superpowers on a treaty to prevent the militarization of space. This move came as something of a surprise because Soviet spokesmen, in a vain effort to roll back the INF deployments begun the preceding fall, had previously insisted that the renewal of negotiations over strategic and intermediate-range nuclear weapons was contingent on the reversal of the INF deployments. The United States responded to Chernenko's offer by insisting that any negotiations over the militarization of space would also have to deal with offensive nuclear weapons, a position that the new general secretary was still unwilling—or more likely, unable—to accept.[5] During 1984 the Soviet negotiating strategy thus failed to produce positive results on either INF or SDI.

The dilemma of how to handle the connection between talks over SDI and negotiations over offensive arms provoked serious disagreement within the Soviet leadership. Despite the official demand for a prior Western commitment to INF rollbacks, Chernenko was so eager to reengage the United States in arms negotiations, particularly over SDI, that he dropped this precondition from his pronouncements on the possibility of new talks. Shortly after becoming general secretary, Chernenko, omitting the demand for rollbacks, issued a public bid for new talks but was promptly corrected by the TASS news agency. After temporarily giving ground on the issue, in early September he again omitted the rollback requirement from a bid for negotiations on space and other arms. Again he was immediately corrected—this time by the Foreign Ministry.[6] The centrality of the rollback issue makes it certain that these discrepancies and subsequent emendations were not simply the product of inadequate coordination within the Soviet policymaking apparatus.

Plainly the leadership was divided over whether to renew the superpower dialogue in order to take up the issue of space weapons. On the same day that the second "clarification" of Chernenko's views appeared, *Kommunist* republished Chernenko's statement without the correction and ran an article that castigated domestic "realists" and "well-intentioned skeptics" who believed it was "naive to think about any sort of future for détente."[7] One target of this criticism was Politburo member Grigorii Romanov, who almost certainly had backed Ogarkov's sustained challenge to prevailing party policy and manifestly doubted that new arms negotiations would yield any benefit. In a speech that did not mention the possibility of further talks, Romanov asserted that U.S. responses to previous Soviet arms-control proposals had been unchangingly negative and that the danger of war was still increasing. Only people who were "naive," he added in a pointed riposte to *Kommunist*, could believe Washington's rhetoric about its peaceful intentions.[8] Politburo member Gorbachev, by contrast, did broach the possibility of renewing bilateral arms talks. Although highly critical of past U.S. negotiating tactics, Gorbachev cited Chernenko's recent expression of willingness to renew negotiations and said that if Washington was prepared to negotiate on equal terms, an improvement in superpower relations "naturally" was possible.[9]

Buoyed, presumably, by such support, Chernenko made yet another unconditional offer for superpower arms talks and finally managed to make his position stick.[10] A day later the Soviet media announced Marshal Ogarkov's transfer from his position as head of the General Staff to an undisclosed post, and the Soviet Union quickly accepted a U.S. invitation for Gromyko to meet with Reagan in Washington.[11] At the end of September Gromyko traveled to the United States, expressed a desire for new arms talks, and, without mentioning the INF deployments, stated vaguely that the United States must "remove the obstacles it has put in the way" of talks.[12] The following month Ogarkov, under obvious duress, publicly reversed his previous views and affirmed the utility of diplomacy as a means of coping with the Western challenge, and Romanov ended speculation about Ogarkov's fate by disclosing that the marshal had been demoted not to the directorship of a military academy, as rumored earlier, but to an important command in the European theater.[13] Apparently Ogarkov's fall from grace was cushioned by his timely recantation and by continued support from some Politburo members. In mid-November Chernenko wrote Reagan a letter on the subject of arms talks, and later in the month the superpowers announced that foreign minister Gromyko and Secretary of State Shultz would start discussions of "new negotiations" on "the whole range of questions concerning nuclear and space weapons."[14]

In January 1985 the United States and the USSR finally agreed on the specific terms for the new cycle of arms negotiations to be held in Geneva. The terms called for the negotiations to be conducted in three parallel sets of talks, dealing respectively with strategic offensive, intermediate offensive, and space weapons. Although the Soviets dropped INF rollbacks as a precondition for the talks, they held firmly to the position that agreements could be reached on INF and strategic offensive weapons only if weapons were simultaneously banned from space. They did not, however, succeed in obtaining an advance U.S. commitment to accept such a ban. The agreement to hold new talks papered over fundamental Soviet-American differences on the relationship between offensive and defensive arms limitations, and parts of the Reagan administration continued adamantly to oppose any linkage between new restrictions on offensive weapons and on SDI.[15]

In the first half of 1985, as the depth of the persisting gap between the Soviet and U.S. positions became evident, there were further hints of internal controversy on the Soviet side. Carefully avoiding a direct challenge to the party leadership, Marshal Akhromeev, the new chief of the General Staff, nevertheless issued an oblique reminder that Soviet military security should not be jeopardized. Akhromeev asserted that if the ABM treaty ceased "for any reasons" to be in force, this would destroy the basis on which negotiations over strategic arms could be conducted, and he offered a historical excursus that may have been meant to show that in the absence of such restraints the party could not afford to neglect strategic defense.[16] At roughly the same time, the resilient Ogarkov published a new pamphlet in which he rescinded much of his recent mea culpa. Once again Ogarkov emphasized the military threat from the West and indirectly questioned the ability of Soviet diplomacy to parry the U.S. buildup. Whatever his relative priorities for Soviet military programs, Ogarkov seemed pessimistic about the possibility of limiting future BMD systems through negotiation. Reviewing the U.S. negotiating positions in the past INF and strategic arms reduction talks (START), he asserted that U.S. ruling circles had shown that "in actuality they do not want any mutually acceptable arrangements.'' In his previous writings Ogarkov had questioned the utility of arms negotiations by listing the many historical instances in which the United States had purportedly rejected Soviet offers to negotiate. His new pamphlet added an item to the list, claiming that in 1958 the United States had rebuffed a Soviet proposal to prohibit the militarization of space. The pamphlet was sent to the typesetter in February 1985, about a month after Gromyko had formally committed the USSR to negotiate over space and other weapons with U.S. representatives at Geneva.[17]

These events shed some light on the evolution of Soviet policy since the Geneva talks got under way in March 1985. In his first months as general secretary, Gorbachev adopted a rather hard public line. Pressing for U.S. agreement to a linkage between limits on SDI and on offensive nuclear arms, he twice hinted strongly that the negotiations might be broken off if the United States failed to comply.[18] In midyear, however, after forcing Romanov, his leading conservative rival, out of the Politburo, Gorbachev began to show more flexibility. At the start of July he confirmed that he had agreed to a summit meeting with President Reagan in the fall, and at the end of the month he announced that a five-month moratorium on Soviet nuclear tests would begin in August, on the anniversary of the atomic bombing of Hiroshima. These steps, incidentally, coincided with some signs that Gorbachev was seeking to limit the growth of Soviet military spending.[19] While the test moratorium was obviously intended to focus political pressure on U.S. military programs, it entailed a genuine cost for Soviet weapons programs as well.[20]

At the same time, Gorbachev attempted to take advantage of differences within the NATO alliance to blunt acceptance of SDI. Rallying the West Europeans against the program, however, has proved a difficult task. During a visit to France in the fall of 1985 Gorbachev tried to line up the government against SDI. His effort was rebuffed, despite the French government's strong reservations concerning BMD. Nor did the Soviet leader manage to exert the intended indirect influence on West German governmental policy through assiduous wooing of the Social Democrats. Although he and his advisers undoubtedly hoped that their efforts would contribute to a Social Democratic victory in the 1987 West German elections, the prospects for such an outcome grew increasingly dim as the election campaign progressed. As of late 1986 the chances for a Labour victory in Britain looked more encouraging, but the British elections were still up to a year and a half away. Thus far, the Soviet attempt to turn Europe against SDI has yielded meager results. In the superpower contest for West European opinion the Reagan administration has used economic blandishments, in the form of agreements to share SDI funds and research findings, to win the approval or at least acquiescence of the British, Italian, and West German governments during the current phase of SDI.

Even if Soviet political appeals evoked a warmer response from Western Europe, they could play no more than a subordinate role in the campaign against SDI. The European antinuclear movement is still politically depleted from its unsuccessful attempt to block the U.S. INF deployments. A vigorous effort to galvanize the movement by actually breaking off superpower arms talks, as the Soviet Union did in the fall of 1983, would run the serious risk that the USSR would be perceived as the major obstruction to arms control. The risks of repeating the walkout tactic are heightened by SDI's lack of concrete political symbols, such as the U.S. missiles and bases that were the focus of the West European opposition to the INF deployments. Still more important, West European attitudes, which were of decisive importance for the U.S. ability to base new intermediate-range missiles in Europe, are not decisive for the continuation of SDI. Even if such West European governments as France persist in opposing SDI, the United States can proceed with the development and deployment of a BMD system—which it could not have done in the case of the INF forces.

For this reason, the Soviet Union has recently concentrated on encouraging domestic U.S. opposition to SDI and convincing U.S. policymakers to conclude a new arms agreement restricting BMD. Although a few Western analysts have suggested that the frustrations of dealing with the Reagan administration may prompt Gorbachev to shift to a "Eurocentric" foreign policy that downgrades the importance of relations with the United States, U.S. military power and the overriding importance of SDI dictate that Soviet diplomacy must continue to center on the United States. Gorbachev cannot afford to adopt a stance of public indifference toward the evolution of U.S. policy. If time was no problem, he could downgrade relations with the United States as a way of "educating" the American public and then propose a new improvement in bilateral ties. Time constraints, however, do not afford such a luxury. The deployment of any new U.S. BMD weapons may still be a decade or more in the future, but in order to be prepared to deploy adequate countermeasures at that time, Soviet policymakers must soon begin making difficult strategic and economic decisions about such steps. Assuming that his aim is to stop SDI before he is compelled to adopt expensive new military programs, Gorbachev must elicit a change of U.S. policy relatively quickly—within, perhaps, two or three years.

Partly for this reason, late in 1985 the Soviet government augmented its political campaign against SDI with dramatic new arms-control proposals. In October Soviet negotiators put forward a proposal that entailed major substantive concessions, as well as provisions manifestly unacceptable to the United States. The offer called for 50 percent reductions in strategic weapons and vehicles, including subceilings that would necessitate sizable cuts in the Soviet ICBM force and considerably reduce the Soviet advantage in ICBM throw weight. This concession, however, was predicated on the prohibition of all SDI research (as well as development and field testing) and on the inclusion of U.S. INF and other forward-based forces in the category of "strategic" weapons.[21]

In the buildup to the November 1985 summit with President Reagan, Gorbachev tried again to extract a U.S. agreement to negotiate restrictions on SDI. At the meeting itself bargaining over whether the final communiqué should include a call for such limits went on until 4:30 A.M. of the last day, but in the end U.S. negotiators refused to acquiesce and the communiqué presented a statement of general principles rather than any concrete agreements. While noting that serious differences remained between the U.S. and Soviet negotiating positions, the document stated that the summit had resulted in "greater understanding" on both sides and a determination to improve bilateral relations. The two leaders also affirmed that a nuclear war between the superpowers could not be won and should never be fought, and each pledged that his country would not seek military superiority over the other. As for arms limitations, the communiqué said the leaders had agreed to accelerate the Geneva negotiations in the hope of achieving "early progress" on such questions as 50 percent reductions in nuclear arms and an interim INF accord. It also called for a second summit "in the nearest future."[22]

In a report shortly after the summit, Gorbachev described the meeting as a political milestone. Despite his forbidding depiction of the U.S. military buildup, he claimed that the passage of the communiqué commiting each side to avoid nuclear war and not to seek military superiority was highly significant. Of course, said Gorbachev, a communiqué was not a formal agreement, but it nevertheless expressed "a fundamental stance of the leaders of both countries obligating [them] to a great deal." The general secretary remarked that the superpowers faced a dangerous turning point in their strategic relations, and he acknowledged that they continued to be at odds over SDI. However, he said, in view of the gravity of the situation "even the smallest chance" to curb the arms race should not be lost. Rather, "especially responsible decisions" were necessary, and "inactivity or slowness in actions" would be "criminal." If the decision to open a dialogue with President Reagan had not been taken, tomorrow it would have been "a hundred times harder," and perhaps even too late.[23] Obviously Gorbachev viewed the summit as part of an urgent political struggle to defeat SDI, and he appeared to be trying to persuade persons who doubted that it had been as successful and significant as he claimed.

Some important party officials were obviously skeptical. Politburo member Shcherbitskii, for instance, paid lip service to the utility of the summit but then recorded a series of important reservations. Even before the meeting, he remarked, it had been clear that the Reagan administration intended to continue to pursue military superiority; recent White House statements, he added, demonstrated that superiority remained the administration's goal. At present, said Shcherbitskii, possibilities for reaching a common understanding with the United States on fundamental questions, particularly SDI and the SALT II agreement, "do not exist."[24] The wording of this passage was striking. Gorbachev had forthrightly acknowledged that the superpowers were at odds over SDI, but he and Reagan had agreed that there was a real prospect of reducing strategic nuclear arms, the weapons covered by the SALT II agreement, and INF forces. By suggesting that agreements on strategic nuclear forces and on INF, which presumably qualified as another "fundamental question," were impossible, Shcherbitskii appeared to be registering opposition to any move to decouple SDI from agreements on offensive nuclear weapons. Nonetheless, the possibility of decoupling INF from SDI was implied in the comprehensive arms-control proposal Gorbachev issued about two months after the summit. The difference between the two Politburo members on this point helps explain why Western commentators found the Soviet position on the INF-SDI linkage ambiguous in late 1985 and early 1986.[25]

Shcherbitskii's reservations about the summit were echoed by some military officials. Marshal Akhromeev praised the "firmness" of the Soviet summit delegation and voiced military support for the previously announced moratorium on additional SS-20 deployments, but he remained silent about the USSR's unilateral moratorium on nuclear testing and remarked that Reagan's commitment at Geneva not to strive for military superiority was "still only words."[26] Shortly afterward, Akhromeev called for more objective evaluation of the potential enemy's military preparations in order to develop timely Soviet military countermeasures.[27] Another military spokesman noted pointedly that unilateral acts of restraint, such as the moratoriums on ASAT and nuclear tests, had elicited nothing from the United States except continued tests of similar weapons. The United States holds more nuclear tests than any other country, continued this writer, and "there are still no other pieces of information besides those which confirm the course taken earlier by Washington toward the creation of space-strike weapons, the quantitative growth and qualitative perfecting of first-strike nuclear systems."[28] No doubt the existence of such views explains why the summit's defenders went out of their way to claim that "only naive simpletons and demagogues" could have asked that the meeting achieve more.[29] Within days the military press, taking its cue from Gorbachev's report, began to laud the results of the summit, but this change of tone only highlighted the unvarnished skepticism of some of the initial accounts.[30]

Gorbachev's viewpoint was spelled out further by an editorial in the party's journal for the indoctrination of military officers. Highlighting SDI, the editorial described a menacing U.S. military challenge backed by a powerful American military-industrial complex, but it used this gloomy picture to justify urgent political steps to defuse the danger. "The creators of SDI already want to do everything to give it so much momentum that by 1988—the year the main advocate of this program will leave the helm of the American ship of state—it will be impossible to stop, even if the idea of 'star wars' is recognized as insufficiently substantial in a military sense."[31] Noting the absence of a unified policy toward the USSR within the Reagan administration, the editorial promised that the USSR would do "everything possible" to counter SDI and then offered an unusually detailed recitation of recent Soviet arms-control proposals.

In sharp contrast to this catalogue of arms-control offers, the journal remained silent about any possibility of Soviet military countermeasures. Claiming that time had proved the "unambiguous conclusion" that the summit had strengthened security, the editorial underscored the two leaders' commitment not to seek military superiority and to speed the negotiations over offensive and defensive arms. It closed with the observation that Gorbachev's final summit statement on international television had made an impact on world public opinion that was "difficult to overestimate."[32] In other words, rather than embark on military countermeasures the USSR should make an immediate, all-out effort to derail SDI by diplomatic means. By marking time diplomatically, the Soviet Union would allow SDI to pick up speed and would lose the chance to affect the American debate over strategic policy during the 1988 presidential elections.

In January 1986 Gorbachev redoubled the campaign against SDI and injected additional novel elements into the Soviet arms-control posture. Bidding to wrest the vision of a nuclear-free world from the proponents of SDI, he unveiled a sweeping proposal for the elimination of nuclear arms by the year 2000 and announced a renewal of the Soviet moratorium on nuclear test explosions. The new proposal, however, was more than just an exercise in public diplomacy. Softening the previous Soviet stance, it offered Soviet-American reductions of intermediate-range nuclear forces while calling for a freeze rather than cuts in the British and French nuclear arsenals. Moreover, the package echoed Gorbachev's past hints that it might be possible to reach an agreement on INF—though not on strategic weapons—before determining the fate of SDI. Two months later Gorbachev directly confirmed that the two issues could be resolved separately.[33]

In addition, in May the Soviet negotiators in Geneva acknowl-edged what other Soviet officials had been informally hinting for some time: they would accept SDI research as part of a new set of limits on BMD but would seek to reinforce the ABM treaty limita-tions on the field testing and deployment of an SDI system. A key proposal was to tighten the terms of the ABM treaty that restrict the testing of exotic ABM systems and to obtain a new agreement under which both sides would be bound not to withdraw from the treaty for a minimum of fifteen to twenty years rather than to adhere merely to the six months' advance notice of withdrawal currently required.[34] Under a strict interpretation of the treaty, this proposal would require the postponement of SDI field tests for at least ten years. It would thereby substantially slow the program and perhaps ultimately halt it through an erosion of domestic American sup-port. If it failed to stop the program, it would still provide a much larger cushion against the possibility of a U.S. "breakout" designed to develop and deploy a space-based BMD system well before Soviet military countermeasures could be implemented.

As an aid to countering SDI through far-reaching arms-control proposals and the unilateral moratorium on nuclear testing, Gor-bachev has tried to make Soviet diplomacy more flexible. A joint Soviet-American test moratorium would benefit the USSR by hampering the development of U.S. offensive nuclear forces and some of the more promising SDI technologies, but the first year of persistent Soviet effort failed to maneuver the Reagan administra-tion into accepting the moratorium.[35] Presumably the hope of achieving this goal was one of Gorbachev's motives for engineer-ing a drastic shake-up of the Soviet diplomatic corps in mid-1986. The shake-up, which strengthened Party Secretary Dobrynin's con-trol of foreign policy, was reportedly intended to make Soviet diplomacy more agile and dispel the image of intransigence from which it had long suffered in the West.[36]

Military men, however, have had doubts about the utility of diplomatic gestures and have apparently resisted the testing moratorium on the grounds that it harms Soviet weapons programs. Evidence for this proposition comes from the timing of renewals of the moratorium as well from Soviet statements. In January 1986 Gorbachev announced that the moratorium would be extended until the end of March; in mid-March a spokesman announced that the moratorium had again been renewed and would be maintained as long as the United States refrained from nuclear tests.[37] Almost simultaneously, Western reports suggested that the Soviet Union was making preparations to resume its own nuclear tests,[38] and after the United States staged a nuclear test near the end of March, Gorbachev made an unsuccessful bid for direct talks with President Reagan to discuss a joint test ban.[39] In mid-April a Soviet statement, alluding to further U.S. tests, stipulated that the USSR would no longer be bound by its earlier commitment not to test, but no Soviet tests occurred and the status of the moratorium remained uncertain.[40] Then, in mid-May, Gorbachev announced that it had been extended to August 6—the anniversary of the bombing of Hiroshima.

Coupled with other evidence, the timing of these announcements suggests that the May renewal of the moratorium was delayed at least partly by internal disagreements.[41] Early in 1986 Marshal Akhromeev, hinting that he was dissatisfied, remarked that unilateral steps such as the test moratorium were "not endless," and the uncertain status of the moratorium in April, accompanied by Soviet preparations to resume tests, probably reflected these sentiments.[42] Three days after Gorbachev announced the May renewal, one proponent of the extension commented that "we prolonged our moratorium, but I am not at all convinced that our military comrades are particularly happy about this."[43] About the same time Dobrynin, in a discussion of the decision to extend the moratorium, referred to the need for "a certain daring" and to "fierce collisions, sharp discussions, and painful disagreements" that had arisen in implementing the new Soviet approach to international affairs.[44] The clear implication of such comments was that some members of the elite did not appreciate the political wisdom underlying the moratorium.

Further signs of internal resistance to the moratorium surfaced in August. Presumably the issue of another renewal arose by late July, when effective international propaganda would have required a new declaration timed to coincide with the August 6 anniversary of the bombing of Hiroshima.[45] However, the new extension was announced only on August 18, thereby sacrificing a valuable opportunity to link the moratorium to the anti-American sentiments aroused in many countries by the memory of Hiroshima. The equivocal efforts of some officials to disprove the existence of internal disagreement over the moratorium served merely to augment the evidence that it existed. Colonel-General Chervov, the General Staff's top specialist on arms control, indignantly denied Western reports of internal Soviet divisions on the matter but then acknowledged "the existence of different opinions and views on these complex issues" within the Soviet elite.[46] Shortly afterward, Akhromeev remarked that the suspension of tests was having a negative impact on Soviet weapons programs and that "we have to face it squarely." Despite the obvious desirability of a firm declaration of military support for the moratorium, Akhromeev did not supply it. In a Soviet television interview he said instead that "as yet it is tolerable to accept a certain degree of detriment," without indicating whether the moratorium met this criterion.[47]

Evidently, members of the military and political leadership have also opposed other aspects of Gorbachev's approach to arms control. About the same time that Soviet negotiators in Geneva offered further concessions on offensive nuclear arms in exchange for limits on SDI, an article by Dobrynin hinted broadly at internal Soviet resistance to offensive reductions. In his exposition of the requirements of the "new political thinking" guiding Soviet diplomacy, Dobrynin rebutted "some people" who believe that current nuclear arsenals ensure strategic stability. This, Dobrynin contended, is a "large error" because the arms race is creating a "completely new situation" and steadily shortening the time available for political leaders to make vital decisions during international crises. Dobrynin then condemned unnamed advocates of the idea that existing nuclear arsenals should be maintained because disarmament would heighten international tensions and increase the incidence of conventional wars. On the contrary, he said, by themselves armaments had never made international relations more peaceful but had only made wars more destructive. "Scientists," he remarked pointedly, "know this no less than politicians."[48]

Military men, including Soviet military men, were conspicuously absent from Dobrynin's formula, and attentive readers must have recalled that shortly after the Geneva summit Marshal Akhromeev had asserted that the preservation of peace hinged on increasing the USSR's military might.[49] Together with Dobrynin's unprecedented call for the creation of new civilian centers of military-political expertise inside the Soviet Union,[50] this passage suggests that the party secretary was taking issue with Soviet officers who had expressed doubts about Soviet proposals for drastic reductions in offensive nuclear arms. If the targets of his critique of benighted military thought were Westerners, he had no plausible reason not to name them, since at another point in the article he attacked the Reagan administration directly for its policies.[51]

The conflicting Soviet views of how to manage the military competition with the United States may help account for Soviet conduct at the recent meeting between Gorbachev and President Reagan at Reykjavik. Soviet ambivalence surfaced in the month before the meeting occurred. Gorbachev repeated that it would be an "unpardonable mistake" to delay negotiations and rejected the notion that the USSR should "stand still for two and a half years"—that is, until a new president had taken office.[52] Nonetheless, one newspaper found it necessary to respond to a reader who cited U.S. nuclear and ASAT tests as evidence that the United States was continuing to arm and asked whether the Reykjavik meeting was "at all necessary" and "worth striving for."[53]

When the two leaders met, the Soviet delegation presented a comprehensive arms-control proposal and made major concessions in the course of the negotiations. In addition to proposing major cuts in strategic ballistic missiles and other nuclear weapons, they surprised the American team by offering an unprecedented "zero-zero" trade that would eliminate all the SS–20 missiles targeted on Europe. They also accepted a low ceiling on SS–20s stationed in Asia. At the same time, however, they demanded that the United States agree to postpone testing of SDI components for at least ten years and agree that any decision about introducing new BMD weapons after that date be reserved for a later decision, which would, implicitly, require the consent of both superpowers. When the United States ruled out new limitations on SDI, the Soviets took the position that such limitations were a precondition for agreement not only on strategic but on intermediate-range nuclear forces. They thereby reversed their offer of almost a year's standing to decouple INF from SDI.

At least two explanations for the Soviet recoupling of INF and SDI are possible. It may conceivably have been a policy option, worked out long before the Reykjavik meeting, to arouse Western hopes for an INF agreement and then place the onus for any failure on the Reagan administration's refusal to limit SDI. In other words, Soviet negotiators at Reykjavik sought to curb SDI and, when this proved impossible, implemented a plan to cast the administration in a negative light a month before Americans went to the polls to decide whether the Republican party should retain control of the Senate. This explanation meshes with some other circumstances. The meeting was hurriedly arranged at Soviet initiative, and the U.S. delegation was reportedly given no indication that the Soviets intended to present a detailed package of arms-control proposals. Moreover, during the preceding eighteen months Gorbachev had carefully courted the U.S. Congress, holding talks with several visiting delegations of U.S. legislators, and at his press conference at the end of the Reykjavik meeting he remarked that perhaps the president should "consult the Congress" about the issues discussed in Iceland.[54]

Alternatively, the recoupling of INF and SDI may have been a last-minute policy shift occasioned by internal Soviet dissatisfaction with Gorbachev's sweeping arms-control offers. In his press conference Gorbachev noted that he, as well as President Reagan, had often been asked whether such a meeting was necessary, whether the pace of negotiations was being forced, who was conceding to whom, and who won and lost by holding the meeting. Although he may simply have been alluding to internal discussions of how to handle the diplomatic contretemps provoked by Moscow's arrest of correspondent Nicholas Daniloff, he may also have been referring to broader reservations within the Soviet elite about the wisdom of holding the Reykjavik meeting and about the concessions on offensive arms that Soviet negotiators made there. Sounding an unusual note, Gorbachev remarked that the potential for arms-control agreements could be actualized in the future if in the White House "and in our [Soviet] national leadership we once more think everything over and manifest responsibility."[55] These words implied that Gorbachev and his associates did not fully agree over how far to go toward compromises on arms control.

This interpretation gains plausibility from Soviet statements after the summit. Shortly afterward Central Committee member Valentin Falin gave an interview that clearly suggested that Marshal Akhromeev, the chief Soviet military representative at the Reykjavik meeting, had resisted Gorbachev's proposals to eliminate nuclear missiles. As Falin put it, "If somebody openly expresses his reservations, as was done by Akhromeev, then this should be considered normal. When somebody proposed we should have so-and-so many missiles and then the party leadership proposes a total renunciation of missiles, it is understandable if somebody furiously asks: 'Why? I might know more about these things!' But believe me, it is particularly the military that understands discipline."[56] Meanwhile the Soviet press answered another reader's inquiry asking, "Shouldn't we have just backed down on the issue of SDI? For if documents had been signed. . .on some things at least, the situation would have improved, and not vice versa."[57] After the meeting Soviet officials offered contradictory explanations on whether an INF agreement could in fact be reached independently of an agreement on SDI, and it is possible that not only ordinary newspaper readers but Soviet leaders held differing views on this question.[58] On balance, the comments on the meeting suggest that some Soviet observers felt the USSR had offered too many concessions, while others felt it had offered too few.

Whatever the precise explanation of the shifts in the Soviet position at Reykjavik, Gorbachev will almost certainly continue to hold out the possibility of another superpower summit and will try to use this prospect as a political lever to induce changes in the American position on SDI. Although he blamed the Reagan administration for the failure at Reykjavik to agree on the framework of a sweeping arms-control package, he laid most of the responsibility on Reagan's advisers rather than on the president himself and explicitly rejected the view that the administration was so dominated by the "military-industrial complex" that an acceptable agreement was impossible.[59] Nor are the dramatic Democratic gains in the post-Reykjavik elections and the spate of Soviet-American recriminations about what transpired in Iceland likely to cause Gorbachev to slow the pace of arms-control negotiations and "wait out" the Reagan administration in the hope that the next administration will be easier to deal with.[60]

Although the 1988 presidential campaign will probably offer the Soviets their best foreseeable opportunity to deflect the SDI program by political means, Gorbachev has several reasons for continuing to seek curbs on SDI now. This course of action will strengthen anti-SDI forces in the 1988 presidential campaign, and it may also help Gorbachev avoid decisions he would prefer not to face. To reduce or postpone the need to adopt expensive military counter-measures, Gorbachev must obtain a change of U.S. policy fairly quickly. The beginning of the new U.S. administration will coincide with the preparation of the 13th Five-Year Plan, which will pose sharp choices about the level of military research and production for the period 1991–95, and it might prove difficult to reach a comprehensive arms-control accord in time for it to affect such decisions, even if the new administration is not committed to SDI. In addition, despite SDI's extremely long lead times, Gorbachev and his supporters apparently fear that the program may build up too much political momentum to be stopped after 1988, no matter what the outcome of the elections, and they must be aware that some American conservatives are seek-ing to force the issue by lobbying for new ABM deployments immedi-ately, even before the feasibility of SDI can be determined. Finally, during the late 1980s and early 1990s the United States is scheduled to begin field tests, which, from the Soviet standpoint, will clearly contravene the ABM treaty.[61] Once these tests get underway, the psychology of superpower competition and the politics of Soviet military policymaking are both likely to increase the pressure for Soviet commitments to major new weapons programs.

Gorbachev and like-minded officials thus have a two- to three-year "window of opportunity" in which to negotiate arms agree-ments that encompass SDI. After that time, as U.S. defense plan-ners begin to make specific choices about the shape of a future SDI system and the lead times for devising military countermeasures become shorter, Soviet policymakers are likely to focus increasingly on creating and implementing such military responses. Because internal pressures are already mounting for a shift of emphasis to military programs, Soviet foreign-policy strategists cannot afford to slow their drive to achieve limits on SDI.

In theory, they might go about this in one of several ways. One alternative is to refuse temporarily to participate in arms-control negotiations until the United States affirms the need to limit future BMD development and deployment. The argument in favor of treating limits on SDI as a precondition for negotiations is that it will increase the political pressure on the Reagan administration to place unilateral restraints on SDI.

This approach, however, is at odds with Gorbachev's general approach to diplomacy, which emphasizes flexibility, the appearance of reasonableness, and the ability to converge on an objective from several angles. There is, moreover, the sobering precedent of the failure of such tactics to defeat the INF deployments. Because of its defensive rationale, SDI is harder to depict in negative political terms, and a new walkout from Geneva would therefore prove no more beneficial now than in 1983. It could easily strengthen support for defense spending in the United States, where public enthusiasm for high defense budgets is waning. Moreover, it would compound Gorbachev's domestic political problems because it would create an atmosphere of greater external military danger and strengthen the Soviet military's case for immediate increases in defense expenditures.

A second alternative is to accept the need for negotiations but to refuse to impose limits on offensive arms, strategic or intermediate-range, without an offsetting U.S. agreement to restrict SDI. The advantage of this position is that it satisfies the concern of Soviet conservatives that Soviet negotiators might "concede too much" and would demonstrate to the West that offensive arms control cannot proceed on the basis of "business as usual" if SDI is not restricted. The disadvantage is that this stance will make the USSR look less flexible in the eyes of the American public and may not achieve the apparent Soviet goal of eliciting West European pressure to sacrifice SDI as a means of obtaining cuts in INF.[62]

A third alternative is to reverse field and follow through with the decoupling of INF—but not strategic nuclear forces—from SDI. Reaching an agreement on INF would have the advantage of demonstrating to the American public that the Soviet Union is serious about arms control, but it would also risk creating the impression that the USSR might ultimately accept limits on strategic offensive weapons as well without obtaining restrictions on SDI. Logically, of course, this does not follow. An agreement that entailed dismantling the SS–20s targeted on Europe would not materially affect the Soviet ability to respond to SDI as currently proposed, whereas Soviet ICBMs and SLBMs would be a vital part of the Soviet effort to counter an extensive SDI deployment and retain the ability to devastate the United States through a nuclear strike. Nonetheless, there is a serious possibility that an agreement of this kind could reduce the political pressure on SDI in the United States and validate the fear of some Soviet conservatives that the USSR is losing its credibility in arms negotiations.

In theory, a fourth alternative is to accept limits on offensive strategic arms (as well as on INF) without new restrictions on SDI. Although administration officials have sometimes suggested that the Soviets' profound fear of SDI will lead them to accept drastic cuts in offensive strategic forces while agreeing to the future deployment of BMD systems, this is extremely implausible. Rather, the opposite is likely to occur. The depth of the fear of SDI will lead Soviet negotiators to resist such cuts more strongly than in the past unless they can ensure that BMD systems will continue to be limited. To cut ballistic missile forces without such guarantees would mean sacrificing a necessary means for counteracting a large U.S. BMD system if and when it is deployed.

Moreover, such a measure would be nearly impossible to justify to members of the Soviet political elite. Whatever else one may think about Soviet perceptions of SDI, it is evident that Soviet observers genuinely perceive the initiative as a threat to Soviet security— one with enormous offensive potential. If the SDI program continues to gather momentum in the United States, this will provoke deepening fears within the Soviet national-security establishment. Under such conditions a leader would have to have great political conviction and enormous political strength to conclude an agreement limiting offensive strategic arms even for a limited period. Such a step would strike many military and party officials as an act of weakness and would probably intensify internal demands for the USSR to accelerate the development and deployment of its own BMD system.[63]

Finally, the Soviets might consider negotiating a controlled introduction of BMD systems on both sides. One option would be to negotiate the deployment of ground-based point defenses in both countries but to prohibit the deployment of space-based systems. A possible advantage of such an agreement is that the Soviets clearly regard space-based BMD systems as more destabilizing than ground-based BMD weapons,[64] and in the technologies necessary for ground-based defense the Soviets are considerably stronger relative to the United States than in the technologies that may be used for space-based systems. A further possible advantage is that

Soviet ICBMs, in contrast to U.S. ICBMs, are based close to population centers, so that hard-site defense of these bases might provide
some collateral protection—to the degree such protection is possible—for the Soviet population. For the Soviets, the critical defect
in such a policy is that such a proposal would nevertheless be extremely expensive, and it might open the political floodgates by
accepting the Reagan administration's contention that ballistic
missile defense may be a good thing. Once such a proposal was
made, the Soviets would lose a key instrument in their political
struggle to block SDI. Yet once the Soviet political struggle against
SDI was lost, the Western champions of BMD would be unlikely to
accept half a loaf in the form of terminal-phase defense alone. To
accept such a restriction might well shift the net advantage from
the deployments in favor of the USSR. Moreover, it would mean
that the U.S. advocates of SDI would have to abandon openly the
dream of an effective population defense.

Even more remote is the possibility that the USSR and the
United States might cooperate in a negotiated transition to space-
based BMD systems. Although the official U.S. position toward SDI
calls for a cooperative transition, the Soviets are profoundly skeptical, and with good reason. Although there are persuasive grounds
to doubt that a permanent increase in U.S. security would result
even if such a transition could be achieved,[65] the main point in the
present context is that this sort of transition is extremely unlikely
to occur.

A cooperative transition presupposes either that the Soviets
and Americans deploy their defensive systems in step with one
another or that they somehow prevent the lack of simultaneous
deployment from unleashing an unregulated competition in strategic weapons. Historically, however, the superpowers have not
deployed new types of weapons, such as ICBMs or MIRVs, at
precisely the same time, and these asynchronous deployments have
been a major spur to the arms race. Because space-based weapons
will take an exceptionally long period to develop and will be extremely complex, timing will be an even more serious problem in
this case. No less significant, the complexity and untestability of
the deployed systems will make it extremely difficult to agree on
what components will give each side a comparable BMD capability
at any given stage of the transition. Comparing such systems to

each other will be far more difficult than measuring the controversial trade-offs between accuracy and throw weight that have bedeviled attempts to equalize the Soviet and U.S. offensive nuclear arsenals. This, in turn, will make each side fear that the other may be gaining a disproportionate strategic advantage as the defensive deployments unfold, and it will increase the temptation to initiate the all-out development and deployment of offensive as well as defensive systems.

Because the United States leads in most of the technologies that will be required for space-based weapons, it might in theory cope with these difficulties by slowing the SDI program to match Soviet progress or by sharing U.S. SDI technology with the USSR. Notwithstanding President Reagan's occasional promises to share SDI technology, it will be impossible for the Soviets to place any trust in either possibility. The president's promises clash with his administration's vigorous campaign to restrict Soviet acquisition of technologies having far less military significance, and a sizable number of administration officials oppose the idea of sharing SDI know-how.[66] Even if the Soviets believe in the administration's sincerity, they cannot count on receiving SDI technology, since future U.S. presidents will make many of these decisions. The USSR will not gamble its fate on U.S. goodwill, any more than the United States would gamble on Soviet goodwill in a comparable situation. Rather, the Soviet leaders will prepare militarily to overcome an enlarged U.S. BMD system.

If the U.S. commitment to SDI still seems firm in the late 1980s, the first Soviet military response is likely to be to develop and prepare to deploy effective defense-suppression weaponry that could attack a space-based BMD system directly. Such systems could consist of weapons that would attack either from space, as the current primitive Soviet ASAT is designed to do, or directly from earth, as a ground-based laser might. The advantage of defense-suppression weapons is that they would be relatively inexpensive and might benefit from the ASAT technology that the USSR already possesses. The main disadvantage would be political. By initiating new field tests of ASAT weapons, the USSR would undermine the claim that it wishes to avoid the militarization of space and is not working toward space-based defenses of its own. This, in turn, would strengthen the hand of the Western advocates of SDI.

Soviet policymakers thus face a serious choice about the timing of such a program. If they have not already done so, they will certainly accelerate the laboratory research and development programs required for the creation of more effective space-launched ASAT weapons; one key part of this work will be to develop the sophisticated infrared sensors needed for such a system. They may also step up development work on ground-based lasers. If Soviet advocates of the political strategy continue to prevail, large-scale testing of defense-suppression weapons is unlikely to begin before the end of the 1980s, but if officials favoring military responses gain influence, such tests may begin sooner. Marshal Akhromeev has already pointed out that the treaty permits the testing of a fixed, land-based ABM system based on "other physical principles" and able to protect one region of each country.[67] Such a weapon would still be a far cry from a useful BMD system, but it could be a major step toward an effective defense-suppression weapon for use against a U.S. space-based BMD system.

If SDI moves further along the road from research to deployment, the Soviets will have to decide whether to respond primarily by expanding their offensive nuclear arsenal or creating an extensive BMD system of their own. Judging by Soviet statements, Soviet officials and commentators are already jockeying over which response would be preferable. Gorbachev, for instance, appears to favor offensive over defensive programs. Although he has said that the United States would not be permitted to obtain a monopoly on space-based weapons, he has stressed that the USSR would find a relatively inexpensive response to SDI, and after the Reykjavik meeting he stated flatly that the Soviet response to the deployment of an SDI system would be "asymmetrical." He has also remarked that it would be wrong for the United States "to hope to . . . prompt us to needless expenditures," thereby implying that Soviet policymakers should not overreact and fall into an American trap designed to bankrupt the economy.[68] Taking a similar tack, Party Secretary Dobrynin recently promised that the USSR would counter the creation of an extensive space-based BMD with an answer that is "less expensive and perhaps actualized in a shorter time; by the way, it is not at all required that this answer occur in space."[69] Evidently the two leaders share some civilian specialists' apprehension that the costs of matching the U.S. military buildup, particularly SDI, could injure the economy and harm Soviet national security in the process.[70]

Other officials seem more prepared to try to match SDI with a large Soviet BMD system. When Shcherbitskii came to the United States early in 1985, he asserted that Moscow would respond to the further development of SDI with "both offensive and defensive" measures, leaving the impression that the defensive response would include an extensive Soviet BMD.[71] Marshal Akhromeev has also promised that in case of continued U.S. BMD development the USSR will deploy missile defenses as well as offensive countermeasures, and he has said that if necessary, the Soviet program of economic revitalization would be sacrificed for this end.[72] The tone of this statement differs markedly from Gorbachev's emphasis on devising relatively inexpensive military countermeasures.

Despite pressures to respond to SDI with a large Soviet BMD, the USSR's first major military response will probably be to build an upgraded offensive strategic force that Soviet strategists believe is powerful enough to overwhelm the planned U.S. system. General B. M. Shabanov, the principal overseer of weapons development and procurement at the Ministry of Defense, has stated that the USSR would respond to an extensive U.S. BMD system by "using the same 'new technologies' for the improvement of [Soviet] rockets with the purpose of giving them a capacity to break through the 'space shield' with a counterblow." While alluding to unspecified "other necessary measures" that the USSR might adopt, Shabanov has refrained from suggesting that the USSR would respond by building space-based defenses of its own.[73] Shabanov's silence about Soviet BMD probably reflects a judgment that a sharp upgrading and expansion of offensive nuclear forces would capitalize on the Soviets' heavy past investment of research and resources in such forces and would conserve scarce inputs for the other weapons systems he is responsible for developing. Presumably, officers of the Strategic Rocket Forces and most other services can be counted on to champion such views within the Ministry of Defense and before the Defense Council.

The upgrading of Soviet strategic offensive forces could take several forms. Intensified development of new penetration aids and decoys for offensive missiles would substantially complicate the job of a U.S. BMD system. Another likely measure would be to initiate development of fast-burn boosters able to degrade the capacity of a U.S. space-based BMD system if and when it is deployed. Having overcome most of their past difficulties in engineering the requisite solid-fuel launchers, the Soviets could develop such boosters without a crash effort before a large U.S. BMD system was deployed.[74] They could also deploy decoy boosters without warheads—a measure that would reportedly be relatively economical—and/or increase the number of fully armed offensive missiles.

Despite the heavy pressures on the Soviet military budget, such steps would be quite feasible. Careful analysis does not support those administration officials who claim that the USSR would be unable to accelerate the expansion of its strategic offensive forces in response to SDI. It is quite true that the Soviets are already engaged in a formidable program of modernizing their strategic offensive forces,[75] but this program could be substantially accelerated. According to a study prepared by U.S. intelligence agencies, if the USSR continues to abide by the overall limits established under the SALT II treaty, the number of warheads on Soviet ballistic and cruise missiles is likely to rise from about 9,000 in the mid-1980s to about 12,000 in 1990. However, if the USSR elects not to observe the SALT II limits, it will be able, simply by continuing the current rate of new deployments, to increase the number of nuclear warheads in its weapon inventory to about 16,000 by the mid-1990s. If it elects to speed up the current rate of deployments, the number of warheads could reach at least 21,000.[76] In other words, in considerably less time than the United States would require to deploy an extensive BMD, Soviet strategic planners will have the option of increasing the projected number of nuclear warheads targeted on the United States by at least 60 percent. Moreover, in the absence of treaty restraints the U.S. government will be unable during the next ten years to match potential Soviet offensive deployments without overcoming major U.S. domestic political obstacles and instituting large new offensive programs.[77]

Nor will the Soviet response to SDI necessarily be decided by the "cost-exchange ratio"—that is, the ratio between the cost of one country's military measures and the cost of a rival country's countermeasures to overwhelm them. During the past year relatively cautious administration officials have argued that the United States should deploy an extensive BMD system only if the cost-exchange ratio favors strategic defense over strategic offense, whereas the most convinced advocates of SDI have argued the opposite. Despite its portentous implications for the future of the U.S. SDI, this debate misses a central point about the Soviet decisionmaking calculus. Soviet decisionmakers will compare the relative costs of various Soviet courses of action, not the relative costs of Soviet and U.S. actions. Even if an extensive U.S. BMD system was cheaper than the Soviet steps necessary to overwhelm it, the Soviets would in all likelihood take these steps because the strategic risks of inaction would be unacceptable.[78] Only if the Soviets were absolutely unable to afford additional offensive countermeasures might the cost-exchange ratio, as usually interpreted, legitimately be made a central criterion of U.S. policy. Plainly, however, the USSR can afford to take such countermeasures.

Depending on the lines along which the SDI program evolves, the Soviet offensive programmatic response may also entail expanding the Soviet capability to strike the United States with cruise missiles and with bombers, since a BMD system alone would not protect against such threats. This step might be politically more difficult than the expansion of the ICBM force because it would entail a redistribution of resources from the Strategic Rocket Forces to the navy (for more submarines and submarine-launched cruise missiles) and to the air force, but it would be quite feasible technically. The Soviets are currently developing a new, full-fledged intercontinental bomber, code-named Blackjack, which will start to be deployed around 1989, and they are developing several new types of cruise missiles to augment the air-launched cruise missiles they have already fielded.[79] By increasing the numbers of such air-breathing nuclear systems, the Soviets could pose an enlarged strategic threat to the United States.

As in the case of work on defense-suppression weapons, the timing of steps to expand Soviet strategic offensive forces could be politically important, since some of them would necessitate a clear violation of the limits established by SALT II. If the U.S. government continues to equivocate about its factual adherence to the SALT II ceilings, a public Soviet decision to abandon the agreement and to expand offensive forces could easily cripple the Soviet political campaign against SDI by raising the specter in the United States of a new ''window of vulnerability.'' As far as possible, the

Soviets will probably try to have it both ways by beginning with countermeasures that do not entail a breach of the SALT II ceilings and only later intensifying the expansion of their offensive strategic arsenal.

Although heavier emphasis on defense-suppression and offensive forces will probably be the initial programmatic responses to further U.S. steps toward BMD deployment, in the longer run the Soviets will undoubtedly commit themselves to adopt a large BMD system of their own. The Soviets are likely to take such a step despite the sizable probability that a highly effective BMD system can never be built, because the probability of SDI's success and the consequences of such a success must be judged separately. If the United States succeeded unilaterally in building an effective BMD system, the danger, from the Soviet standpoint, would appear so enormous that it would be completely unacceptable. As a result, the Soviets will be forced to respond to the continued development of U.S. strategic defense technology by widening their own R and D program and preparing, as best they can, for the ultimate deployment of their own extensive BMD system. The first contingent step in this process might involve the more rapid upgrading of land-based BMD technologies, in which the Soviets are relatively strong, followed by an extensive deployment of ground-based ABM installations once it became certain that the U.S. decision to deploy an SDI system could not be reversed. The advantage of ground-based ABM systems is that they could be deployed rapidly and would demonstrate that the USSR possessed its own extensive missile defenses, even if these defenses are not space-based. Deploying an extensive ground-based BMD would help bridge the psychological gap between U.S. deployment of space-based systems and the later Soviet deployment of equally effective space systems, although the early symbolic stationing of relatively ineffectual Soviet systems in space might have a similar psychological effect. At any rate, in the long run the Soviets would also seek to deploy their own space-based BMD. As indicated earlier, each step in this direction would inflict progressively higher economic costs and political pressures on the Soviet system, but there can be no doubt that in the absence of U.S. restraint the Soviet leadership will launch and attempt to carry out such a program.

# 6.
# U.S. POLICY AND THE FUTURE OF THE SUPERPOWER ARMS COMPETITION

$\mathbf{B}$roadly speaking, the Strategic Defense Initiative has four possible justifications. SDI's proponents sometimes assert that the USSR is already committed to developing and deploying an extensive BMD system and that SDI is merely a U.S. effort to stay abreast of Soviet military progress. Alternatively, it is sometimes said that the United States can achieve greater security, for the USSR as well as for itself, by steering a reluctant Soviet regime into a world dominated by strategic defenses rather than by offensive nuclear weapons. Another alternative, rarely voiced in public but sometimes espoused in private, is that the United States can outstrip the USSR technologically and will therefore gain a decisive strategic advantage from an unregulated race in BMD and space-based weaponry. A contrasting justification is that SDI might be used as a bargaining chip to gain U.S. strategic benefits through tightened restrictions on Soviet offensive and defensive weapons.

Although wartime experiences and Soviet military doctrine predispose the USSR to favor strong strategic defenses, a careful examination of the evidence does not support the claim that the USSR is already committed to developing and deploying a large BMD system. Since the late 1960s most Soviet policymakers have recognized that the construction of such a system would entail major drawbacks for the Soviet Union. These include the enormous cost and dubious technical feasibility of building an effective system; the availability of relatively inexpensive countermeasures; the prospect that America's overall technological superiority might enable it to win a defensive competition even if the USSR initially took the lead; the uncontrolled nature of the accelerated arms race that would ensue; and, finally, an increasing recognition that a mutual capacity for assured destruction, although far from appealing, does exist and can help stabilize the U.S.-Soviet military relationship in times of crisis.

Viewed in the light of Soviet discussions of BMD, Soviet weapons programs appear less ominous than abstract speculation about Soviet motives might suggest. The USSR is conducting research on particle-beam and laser technology with potential applications to space weaponry, and over the past two decades it has slowly developed a primitive ASAT capability. It is also continuing to deploy upgraded surface-to-air missiles for use against enemy aircraft and is developing antitactical ballistic missiles. However, the evidence examined in this book strongly suggests that the principal motivation for Soviet work on BMD and space weapons is to guard against the contingency of an unexpected technological breakthrough followed by a sudden American deployment of an extensive BMD system. Soviet officials are more apprehensive than enthusiastic about the possible strategic consequences of new BMD weapons. Similarly, such Soviet "gray-area" weapons as the SAMs and prospective ATBMs do not constitute calculated violations of the ABM treaty, and they will not produce a major improvement in the USSR's marginal capacity to defend against strategic missile attacks. Construction of the Abalakovo radar, the USSR's one clear violation of the ABM treaty, was an aberration from the general pattern of Soviet compliance with the treaty, and the Soviet LPARs begun since Abalakovo satisfy treaty requirements.[1] The Abalakovo installation was probably not intended to improve the Soviet BMD capacity substantially, and it certainly will not do so.

Despite the Abalakovo violation, the USSR has observed the ABM treaty provisions that are vital to U.S. security, and in the absence of an enlarged U.S. BMD system Soviet policymakers have strong incentives to improve their record of compliance. Most officials believe that an independent decision to deploy a large Soviet BMD system in the foreseeable future would be a mistake. If anything, the USSR today feels more trepidation about an unrestrained competition in BMD than it did twenty years ago, and there is no likelihood of a reversal of the superpowers' economic and technological fortunes sufficient to change this attitude during the next ten or fifteen years. Fearful of losing a race in space-based weapons, the USSR has taken such initiatives as the four-year moratorium on Soviet ASAT testing and the unilateral moratorium on nuclear test explosions. These measures, which entail genuine sacrifices in the development of Soviet military capacities, constitute an attempt to elicit a reciprocal U.S. decision against building an extensive BMD system. The United States thus has a real opportunity to prevent the deployment of any large BMD system, Soviet as well as American, for a long time.

Although the United States has such an option, SDI can still be justified if it will facilitate a cooperative superpower transition to a more secure world of space-based defenses. This alternative rationale for the program rests on the critical assumption that the United States can persuade the USSR to follow a U.S. scenario involving fundamental changes in the military doctrines and weapons systems of both countries. Relying on a schematic interpretation of Soviet military doctrine, some SDI proponents have asserted that the Soviet leadership privately accepts the logic of a defense-dominant world but has masked this acceptance with propaganda designed to obstruct the American program. Therefore, they have argued, it will be possible to induce the USSR to make a transition to a strategic relationship based primarily on ballistic missile defenses.[2]

Although superficially plausible, this forecast involves a wholesale dismissal of Soviet pronouncements that is little short of breathtaking. It is true that the Soviets have sometimes misrepresented their real attitudes toward SDI. However, a decision to ignore Soviet statements exposes Western analysts to the grave ethnocentric risk of assuming that whatever seems strategically desirable in the West is also desirable from the Soviet standpoint. Rather than dismiss Soviet political and strategic thought, Western observers should subject it to rigorous analysis. A systematic effort to understand the Soviet perspective yields persuasive evidence, including evidence drawn from confidential Soviet military sources, that during the past two decades most Soviet officials have come to regard the deployment of space-based BMD systems as a profound threat to Soviet security.

Some SDI advocates take Soviet apprehensions more seriously but believe they can be dispelled through a superpower dialogue that demonstrates that a cooperative transition to extensive BMD systems will increase Soviet security. Viewed against the backdrop of past American debates over arms control, the supposition that U.S. negotiators can bring about such an alteration in Soviet strategic attitudes is ironic. In the 1970s one of the principal U.S. criticisms of the SALT agreements was that U.S. negotiators had naively assumed they could convince Soviet military planners to adopt the U.S. concept of mutual assured destruction.[3] Now, however, some of the same persons who condemned American naïveté during the 1970s propose to work a change in Soviet strategic thought far more radical and visionary than the one that U.S. negotiators sought during the SALT negotiations.

During the 1970s many Soviet officials did gradually accept the notion that mutual assured destruction could stabilize superpower relations in times of crisis, but they were swayed not so much by American arguments as by independent analysis of the strategic situation facing their country. In the second half of the decade prevailing Soviet political and military opinion explicitly recognized the devastating consequences of nuclear war as well as the stabilizing effects of mutual nuclear vulnerability.[4] The record, however, also shows that the change of views did not occur easily. Many Soviet observers made the shift reluctantly, and a few military commentators, exemplified by Bondarenko, resisted it.

The dynamics of this gradual alteration of Soviet strategic thought suggest that the effort to persuade the Soviets of SDI's strategic benefits is likely to fail. The SALT agreements signed during the 1970s were based on theories about the strategic implications of existing armaments whose military capabilities were understood reasonably well, whereas the future capabilities of space-based weapons remain in the realm of speculation. This circumstance alone will make the attempt to reach a common strategic outlook with the Soviets far more difficult than it was during the 1970s. A further complication is that the proponents of SDI are urging the USSR to accept strategic concepts which directly contradict the concepts that U.S. negotiators advocated only a decade ago and which the Soviets slowly adopted through an extended reassessment of their own traditional military postulates. Moreover, today, compared with the late

1960s, fewer senior Soviet and U.S. officials have overlapping attitudes toward BMD. At the beginning of the SALT process some Soviet officials already shared the prevailing U.S. view that BMD would not only speed up the arms race but also complicate the resolution of U.S.-Soviet military crises; today virtually all Soviet officials oppose the American notion that space-based BMD can have a beneficial impact on superpower relations.

Under these conditions an attempt to compel the USSR to accept a joint transition to space-based BMD is more likely to destroy nuclear arms control than to strengthen it. In one sense SDI has enhanced the possibilities for meaningful control of offensive nuclear arms because it has made the USSR more interested in arms restraints than ever before. The evolution of the Soviet negotiating posture during the past two years suggests that the Soviets are now prepared to agree to major cuts in offensive arms. The record, however, also suggests that they will make such concessions only in exchange for strengthened curbs on BMD and space-based weapons. Without such curbs Soviet policymakers are extremely unlikely to agree to any limitations, not to mention reductions, of offensive strategic arms. Instead they will probably launch an accelerated drive to develop ASAT and other defense-suppression weapons and will drastically upgrade their strategic offensive forces while moving toward deployment of a large BMD system of their own. Under these conditions, the superpower dialogue over arms control may well come to an end.

Whether one regards this as a threatening prospect depends on one's attitude toward the progress of military technology. Although a thorough discussion of the implications of various weapons systems goes beyond the boundaries of this book, it seems likely that limitations on the development of new ASAT weapons, which would be closely related to some prospective forms of BMD weaponry, would enhance U.S. security. Because satellites currently serve a vital function in warning of potential enemy missile attacks and would play an important role in guiding counterattacks, they constitute a crucial part of each side's strategic forces, even though they are not weapons per se. If the superpowers' strategic "eyes," which are potentially far more vulnerable than the weapons themselves, become susceptible to sudden destruction, this will introduce a dangerous new measure of instability into Soviet-American strategic relations. The deployment of sophisticated ASAT systems could increase each side's vulnerability to surprise attack and shorten the time available for careful decisions about retaliation against an apparent enemy strike.[5] Aside from the early-warning function, differences in the relative strategic value of Soviet and American satellites in performing other military functions suggest that the United States will be more secure if sophisticated ASAT weapons are not deployed.[6]

A decision to deploy space-based BMD weapons will probably have consequences that are similar but still more far-reaching. Space-based weapons will have a capacity to attack not only missiles but other objects in space. This means that if both sides deploy space-based defenses, each may conceivably acquire the ability to destroy a substantial portion of the other's defenses through a direct strike against its space assets, thereby drastically altering the relative strength of the two sides' military forces.[7] To the degree that strategic defenses become a critical ingredient in the military balance between the superpowers, this vulnerability will increase the instability of their military relationship. The instability would be compounded by deep reductions in strategic offensive arms, because under such conditions the side that struck first would have a correspondingly greater possibility of intercepting enough of the enemy's retaliatory blow to escape overwhelming destruction.[8]

Although we cannot foresee what capacities space-based weapons may ultimately possess, they will undoubtedly have some direct offensive applications, as U.S. officials have begun obliquely to acknowledge since the Reykjavik meeting.[9] Strikes from space platforms against aircraft in flight are likely to become technically feasible, and the possibility of strikes against terrestrial targets, though much harder to gauge, may also become a reality. In view of these possibilities, it is vitally important to examine systematically the potential consequences of deploying offensive as well as defensive weapons in space.

Among the inviting targets for direct attacks from space would be the ground-based radars and communications systems necessary for early warning and control of retaliatory missile strikes, together with the airborne emergency command posts from which national leaders might attempt to direct a general war. A future generation of space-based weapons may be able to destroy such targets without even the slight warning and time for decision currently afforded by ballistic missile flight trajectories.[10] If this seems a fantasy, it is worth recalling that the development and deployment cycle of some of the prospective space-based weapons currently being discussed is upwards of thirty years, and that in a period only slightly longer the superpowers have already moved from reliance on propeller-driven aircraft with conventional bombs to vast inventories of nuclear weapons possessing nearly inconceivable precision and destructive power. Needless to say, a sharp increase in the vulnerability of command and control installations to surprise attack would have a deeply destabilizing effect on the superpowers' military relations, particularly in times of crisis.

Once the weaponization of space commences, cooperative regulation of the process is likely to be even more difficult than the already formidable task of regulating weapons based on earth. If the introduction of space weapons does inaugurate a qualitatively new stage in offensive military capabilities, by the time this fact becomes indisputable it will almost certainly be too late to turn back. The prevention of this eventuality depends on the existence of thresholds that allow the unambiguous verification of each country's military capabilities. After weapons are introduced into space, verification of their capabilities is likely to become extremely difficult, and probably impossible.

This brings us to the third major rationale for SDI—the proposition that an unregulated race in space will enable the United States, through its superior technological prowess, to improve its security position vis-à-vis the Soviet Union. There can be no doubt that today the United States enjoys a substantial lead over the USSR in most fields of technology with potential military applications. Nor can there be any doubt that the United States, if it bends all its efforts to the task, will be able to deploy space-based defenses at any given level of effectiveness well before the USSR can. In the United States, however, the main impediment to the development of weapons is not technological but political. SDI has an extraordinarily long time horizon, and even if it proves feasible technically, future administrations may lack the determination or political power to carry it through. The Soviet Union, by contrast, is technologically weaker but politically dogged. It is therefore conceivable that the United States could pursue SDI long enough to provoke an enduring Soviet response but not long enough to bring the American program to fruition. The outcome might well be a strategic situation less advantageous to the United States than the one that exists today.

Even if the United States maintains SDI's momentum and rapidly deploys the resulting weapons, the ultimate consequences of space-based BMD will in all probability outweigh any shorter-term gains. As we try to imagine the future, we must beware of the soothing assumption that the strategic competition between the superpowers will cease once the United States deploys a space-based defense.[11] The competition is virtually certain to continue at an accelerated pace, and this prospect demands that American policymakers ponder what may happen in the stages that follow U.S. BMD deployments. Although daunting, the prospect of a rapid expansion of the Soviet ballistic missile arsenal is but one of the possibilities requiring attention. Assuming that the United States enjoyed a monopoly on space weapons for the first decade or longer, how should this temporary advantage be weighed against the subsequent Soviet acquisition of similar weapons and the destabilizing effects this situation would produce? In particular, if BMD developments pave the way for powerful space-based weapons able to strike the earth, would we wish the Soviet Union to acquire such weapons, and how would the mutual possession of such capabilities affect the likelihood of general war? Thanks partly to the defensive rationale advanced for SDI, the recent American debate has scarcely broached, let alone answered, these vital strategic questions.

If such issues do not receive attention now, the development of technology—Soviet as well as American—may render them moot. It is probably more than coincidence that Gorbachev, in his press conference after the Reykjavik meeting, made an aside which may have contained a delicate hint that the USSR has the potential to develop its own offensive space weapons.[12] Thanks to the different technical requirements of attacking enemy missiles in flight and attacking terrestrial targets, the deficiencies of Soviet technology may constitute a smaller barrier to the creation of such weapons than to the creation of space-based BMD.[13] Despite the Soviet economic system's many technological flaws, Western analysts would be mistaken to assume that the USSR will prove unable, over the long run, to obtain and deploy weapons comparable to those devised in the United States. This judgment is not supported by the history of conventional weapons, of the atomic and hydrogen bombs, of ballistic missiles, or of MIRVs. Although correct in a narrow sense, Americans who celebrate only U.S. technological dynamism and superiority over the USSR reflect an outlook that future historians may judge to be as politically shortsighted as Nikita Khrushchev's triumphant proclamations of Soviet technological superiority in the 1950s. Over the long term, it is quite likely that the attempt to capitalize on U.S. technological superiority by deploying space-based weapons will lead to a strategic situation that will sharply reduce rather than increase U.S. military security.

If it is true that the United States has compelling reasons to prevent the introduction of weapons into space, then the main value of SDI is as a hedge against unpredictable Soviet behavior and a bargaining chip in superpower arms negotiations. It follows that the United States should be prepared to scale down SDI and pursue further BMD research on a contingency basis only. For reasons of prudence, U.S. BMD research should not be entirely abandoned. As shown above, since the signing of the ABM treaty some influential Soviet officers have maintained that BMD will eventually become technologically feasible, and a few air defense officials have actively pushed for a decision to build such a system. Although this view has not been accepted by the top party leadership, it coincides with the long-standing Soviet enthusiasm for the general idea of strategic defense, and if the feasibility of BMD improved radically during the next decade or two, it might gain a more receptive hearing in Soviet ruling circles. The United States can best ensure that this does not occur by maintaining a limited program of laboratory research to maintain its lead in most of the technologies that might be employed in future BMD systems.

At the same time, the United States should quickly make use of the Soviet fear of SDI to strengthen existing limits on offensive as well as defensive armaments. In launching SDI the Reagan administration has created a bargaining chip of extraordinary value—if the administration will trade it. The offer to restrict SDI should be used to obtain major offensive nuclear cuts that reduce the size of the Soviet arsenal and are structured to increase crisis stability. In addition to such reductions, the United States should pursue tighter restrictions on Soviet gray-area weapons. These restrictions should spell out clearer definitions of permissible and impermissible radar installations and impose tighter limits on Soviet SAM and ATBM programs. The Soviets may resist SAM limits because they face an increasing air-breathing threat from U.S. cruise missiles and from the Stealth bomber now under development. They may also resist limits on ATBMs, which they have developed largely as a defense against Pershing II missiles and are now preparing to deploy. Nevertheless, the threat posed by SDI is so large that the Soviets will probably make concessions on the SAM issue as well as on ATBMs, particularly if the superpowers reach an INF agreement providing for drastic reductions in the Pershing IIs.[14] In exchange for Soviet offensive and defensive concessions the United States should reaffirm the principles of the ABM treaty and accept tighter definitions of critical treaty concepts, such as ABM testing and ABM components, as well as a longer period of notification of withdrawal from the treaty. This step would reassure Soviet leaders and strategic planners that the United States does not intend to transform its own research findings into an extensive BMD system unless the USSR first embarks upon such a course.

The choices now facing U.S. policymakers vividly demonstrate that strategy in the nuclear era depends on judgments that cannot be fully grounded in prior historical experience. Far more than in the prenuclear age, decisionmakers must base policy on hypothetical strategic theories and uncertain judgments about the theories' likely consequences.[15] At the same time, officials must take into account a widening array of arcane technical and political data, including data about a rival superpower whose views and motives are often as difficult to fathom as to trust.

Given the intellectual complexity and grave implications of such decisions, it is hard to envy the persons who must make them, and modesty befits outside observers no less than high officials. It is not too much to insist, however, that a wise U.S. policy toward strategic weapons must rest on a rigorous examination of Soviet policies, views, and options with regard to BMD. The findings of this book suggest that American decisions about SDI may constitute a critical turning point in superpower relations which entails enormous opportunities but also enormous risks, and that American hopes for a unilateral solution to the problem of security in the nuclear age are illusory. If the dire fears about "space-strike weapons" come true for the Soviet Union, sooner or later they will probably come true for the United States as well.

# NOTES

## Chapter 1

1. Some of the scholarship from which this report has benefited are Sayre Stevens, "The Soviet BMD Program," and particularly Raymond L. Garthoff, "BMD and East-West Relations," in Ashton B. Carter and David N. Schwartz, eds., *Ballistic Missile Defense* (Washington, D.C.: The Brookings Institution, 1984), 182–220, 275–329; Mary C. FitzGerald, "The Other Side of SDI: What Does Moscow Say?" in Graham Vernon, ed., *Soviet Perceptions of War and Peace* (forthcoming); Mary C. FitzGerald, "The Soviet Military on SDI," *Soviet Armed Forces Review Annual*, 10 (forthcoming); David Holloway, "The Strategic Defense Initiative and the Soviet Union," *Daedalus* 114, no. 3 (Summer 1985), 257–79; Stephen M. Meyer, "Soviet Strategic Programmes and the US SDI," *Survival*, (November/ December 1985), 274–92; and Rebecca V. Strode, "Space-Based Lasers for Ballistic Missile Defense: Soviet Policy Options," in Keith B. Payne, ed., *Laser Weapons in Space: Policy and Doctrine* (Boulder, Colo.: Westview Press, 1983), 106–61. Useful earlier writings on Soviet strategic defense and military activities in space include Michael J. Deane, *The Role of Strategic Defense in Soviet Strategy* (Washington, D.C.: Advanced International Studies Institute, 1980); Lawrence Freedman, "The Soviet Union and 'Anti-Space Defence,' " *Survival*, no. 1 (January 1977); Stephen M. Meyer, "Anti-satellite Weapons and Arms Control: Incentives and Disincentives from the Soviet and American Perspectives," *International Journal* (Summer 1981), 460–84; and Stephen M. Meyer, "Space and Soviet Military Planning," in William J. Durch, ed., *National Interests and the Military Use of Space* (Cambridge, Mass.: Ballinger Publishing Co., 1984).

2. See, for instance, Kenneth Adelman, "Why Mr. Reagan is Right About SALT," *The New York Times*, June 15, 1986, 2.

3. For example, opponents of SDI have sometimes accepted at face value Soviet statements that SDI is doomed to fail because the USSR can easily match any U.S. achievement in this realm.

4. An official U.S. analysis published in 1985 asserted that "the aggregate of current Soviet ABM and ABM-related activities suggests that the USSR may be preparing an ABM defense of its national territory." (*Soviet Strategic Defense Programs* [Washington, D.C.: U.S. Department of State, 1985], 5.) After the Reykjavik summit, President Reagan stated unequivocally, "For some years now . . . the Soviets have been developing a nationwide defense. They have installed a large modern radar at Krasnoyarsk which . . . is a critical part of a radar system designed to provide radar guidance for anti-ballistic missiles protecting the entire nation." ("Text of Reagan's Broadcast Address on Talks with Gorbachev in Iceland," *The New York Times*, October 14, 1986, A10. The Krasnoyarsk radar is discussed in chap. 3 below.)

5. The need to pay close attention to context is shown by the official U.S. analysis of Soviet doctrine toward strategic defense. The analysis quotes from *Voennaia strategiia*, an authoritative Soviet military treatise published during the 1960s, which asserts that it has become "necessary to assure, essentially, 100 percent destruction of all attacking airplanes and missiles." (Quoted in *Soviet Strategic Defense Programs*, 7.) However, the U.S. publication fails to recognize that such statements disappeared from the most authoritative Soviet military writings after the USSR decided to join with the United States to limit the development and deployment of ABM systems. In the mid-1980s Soviet military theorists have explicitly repudiated many of the general strategic principles enshrined in *Voennaia strategiia*. (James M. McConnell, *Analyzing the Soviet Press—Spot Report No. 1: The Irrelevance Today of Sokolovskiy's Book 'Military Strategy'* [Washington, D.C.: Center for Naval Analyses, May 1985.])

6. During the 1960s a concentration on Soviet doctrinal statements and incipient military programs caused some U.S. government analysts to make serious misjudgments about the likely scale of Soviet BMD deployments in the 1970s. According to one account, an American National Intelligence Estimate (NIE) prepared in 1963 predicted that by 1978 the Soviet BMD system would be expanded to protect all major cities with 500 to 1,000 launchers per city. Another source states that the NIE projected a nationwide total of up to 2,000 long-range ABM interceptors and 6,000 to 8,000 short-range interceptors. Later in the 1960s a vigorous controversy occurred within the U.S. intelligence community over the character of the Soviet ABM program, and some agencies adopted more modest estimates of its likely scope. However, in 1970, when the USSR had installed 64 ABM missiles around Moscow but had suspended further work on the system, one military intelligence branch was reportedly still predicting that 7,000 to 9,000 ABM missiles would be deployed within a few years. (John Prados, *The Soviet Estimate: U.S. Intelligence Analysis & Russian Military Strength* [New York: Dial Press, 1982], 155–64; Jeffrey T. Richelson, "U.S. Intelligence and Soviet Star Wars," *Bulletin of the Atomic Scientists* 42, no. 5 [May 1986], 13.)

It is only fair to note that the 1963 estimate was formulated in an early phase of the Soviet ABM program, when concrete information on the weapons was extremely difficult to obtain and when Soviet politicians and generals were making sweeping assertions about the effectiveness of the ABM weapons then being devised. Moreover, the Soviet government was already engaged in a dramatic expansion of its air defense system. On the other hand, by 1961 U.S. satellite reconnaissance had shown that Khrushchev's earlier military boasts had enormously exaggerated the level of the Soviet buildup in offensive nuclear missiles and that the "missile gap" that did exist favored the United States, not the Soviet Union. Careful consideration of this experience might have led U.S. intelligence analysts to appraise Soviet ABM claims in a different light, as a declaratory substitute for assertions about the offensive balance that the United States had now disproved and publicly rejected.

7. For instance, Ambassador Paul Nitze, chief arms-control adviser to Secretary of State Shultz, has remarked that the Soviet strategic defense effort has "proceeded completely free from the debates of the sort that are occurring now in the West over the utility and implication of our program." (Quoted in Charles Mohr, "Soviet Antimissile Efforts Listed," *The New York Times*, October 5, 1985, 4.) Making the same assumption, some Western academic studies have mistakenly interpreted Soviet minority views for policy. This is true, for example, of two particularly important books (by Bondarenko and Zimin et al.) discussed in chap. 2. For a fairly typical Western interpretation of these works, see Deane, *The Role of Strategic Defense in Soviet Strategy*, 22, 78–80.

8. Robert Tucker, *SDI and American Foreign Policy* (Boulder, Colo.: Westview Press, forthcoming). A classical example is the 1960s calculation by the U.S. Department of Defense that U.S. retaliatory forces would have to be able to destroy approximately one half of the Soviet population in order to deter a Soviet nuclear attack on the United States. Despite its apparent precision, this criterion was based on pivotal assumptions about the political values of the Soviet leadership (as well as on certain judgments about U.S. budgetary possibilities and U.S. domestic political requirements.) In the 1970s critics of U.S. nuclear strategy such as Richard Pipes appraised the Soviet leadership's values very differently. They therefore concluded that the prospect of large population losses might not effectively deter the USSR. (Gregg Herken, *Counsels of War* [New York: Alfred A. Knopf, 1985], 153–54, 229–30, 277–78; Richard Pipes, "Why the Soviet Union Thinks It Could Fight and Win a Nuclear War," *Commentary* 64, no. 2 [July 1977], 21–34.)

9. "No segment of this [military] literature is specifically aimed at foreign readers; the principal target is domestic. It is a peculiar form of inflated Western self-esteem that turns a literature read for profit in the Soviet Union into a performance for its own benefit. Moscow is, of course, aware of alien eavesdropping; hence, much of the rigid propaganda conventions, the misleading statements, the guarded language that borders on the opaque. The substance of the message is not affected, however; the Kremlin cannot afford to deceive its own cadres. If disinformation be defined as a communication that the Soviet elite, skilled in reading the literature of its specialty, would declare to be an untruth, then there is very little disinformation in the Soviet press." (James M. McConnell, "Shifts in Soviet Views on the Proper Focus of Military Development," *World Politics* 37, no. 3 [April 1985], 319.)

10. The main sources of this kind utilized in the present report are *Kommunist (Communist)*, the party's main theoretical journal; *Pravda (Truth)*, the daily party newspaper; and *Izvestiia (News)*, the government daily.

11. This report draws on the following sources of this type: *Krasnaia zvezda (Red Star)*, *Voenno-istoricheskii zhurnal (Military-Historical Journal)*, and *Zarubezhnoe voennoe obozrenie (Foreign Military Review)*, all of which are published by the Soviet

Ministry of Defense; *Vestnik protivovozdushnoi oborony (Air Defense Herald)*, published by the Air Defense Forces; *Kommunist Vooruzhennykh Sil (Communist of the Armed Forces)*, published by the Main Political Administration, a joint party-military organization; *SShA: ekonomika, politika, ideologiia (USA: Economics, Politics, Ideology)*, published by the Institute of the USA and Canada of the USSR Academy of Sciences; and numerous specialized Soviet books.

12. Raymond L. Garthoff, "Mutual Deterrence and Strategic Arms Limitation in Soviet Policy," *International Security* (Summer 1978), 117, 146. Copies of a sizable number of issues of *Military Thought (Voennaia mysl')* were obtained by the U.S. government. At present, the government has declassified issues published before 1974. Regretably, it has not declassified the more recent issues, whose contents might shed considerable additional light on Soviet thinking about BMD.

13. The introduction of weapons into space must be clearly distinguished from the military use of space for other purposes. Ever since the early 1960s the superpowers have increasingly relied on space satellites to provide reconnaissance information, military communications, and early warning of possible enemy attacks. With the limited exception of primitive antisatellite weapons, however, the superpowers have not developed weapons intended to attack targets in space or to be launched from space against terrestrial targets. Ballistic missiles, though they pass through space, are launched from earth.

**Chapter 2**

1. Bruce Parrott, *Politics and Technology in the Soviet Union* (Cambridge, Mass.: MIT Press, 1983), 192–202, 242–43, 251–55; Grey Hodnett, "Ukrainian Politics and the Purge of Shelest," paper prepared for the annual meeting of the Midwest Slavic Conference, Ann Arbor, Michigan, May 5–7, 1977.

2. On the change in growth rates, see U.S. Congress, Joint Economic Committee, *Allocation of Resources in the Soviet Union and China—1984: Part 10* (Washington, D.C.: GPO), 55–56. For Grechko's resistance, see Andrei Grechko, *Vooruzhennye Sily Sovetskogo gosudarstva*, 2d ed. (Moscow: Voenizdat, 1975), 7, 82–83, 92–93, 100, 190–93, and chap. 3 below.

3. Garthoff, "Mutual Deterrence and Strategic Arms Limitation in Soviet Policy," 142–43; Thomas N. Bjorkman and Thomas J. Zamostny, "Soviet Politics and Strategy Toward the West: Three Cases," *World Politics* 36, no. 2 (January 1984), 203–4. For the foot-dragging, see note 44 in chap. 3 below.

4. Arnold L. Horelick and Edward L. Warner III, "U.S.-Soviet Nuclear Arms Control: The Next Phase," in Arnold L. Horelick, ed., *U.S.-Soviet Relations: The Next Phase* (Ithaca, N.Y.: Cornell University Press, 1986), 228.

5. In May 1982, when the administration finally agreed to new strategic arms reduction talks (START), it tabled a proposal that "would have required the Soviet Union radically to restructure its strategic forces and to retire over half of its newly acquired fourth-generation MIRVed ICBMs. In return, the United States offered,

at most, to scale back somewhat a few planned U.S. programs." (Horelick and Warner, "U.S.-Soviet Nuclear Arms Control," 228.)

6. The Carter administration declined to resume the ASAT talks after the Soviet invasion of Afghanistan but continued negotiations on a comprehensive test ban until November 1980, pending a review by the newly elected administration. In mid-1982 the Reagan administration announced that the test ban negotiations would not be resumed. (Warren Heckrotte, "Verification of Test Ban Treaties," in William C. Potter, ed., *Verification and Arms Control* [Lexington, Mass.: D. C. Heath, 1985], 71.)

7. *XXVI s"ezd KPSS: stenograficheskii otchet* (Moscow: Politizdat, 1981), 21, 38–40; Iu. V. Andropov, "Leninizm—neischerpaemyi istochnik revoliutsionnoi energii i tvorchestva mass," *Pravda*, April 23, 1982, 1–2, and *Izbrannye rechi i stat'i*, 2d ed. (Moscow: Politizdat, 1983), 264–65; Konstantin Chernenko, "Po-leninski zhit', rabotat', borot'sia," *Kommunist*, no. 9, 1984, 3–4; M. S. Gorbachev, "Bessmertnyi podvig sovetskogo naroda," *Kommunist*, no. 8, 1985, 16–17.

8. Foreign-policy specialists' disagreement over this point was illustrated in 1982 when a section of the USSR Academy of Sciences convened a large symposium to discuss the military-political strategy of the Reagan administration. See "Formirovanie voenno-politicheskoi strategii administratsii Reigana," *SShA: ekonomika, politika, ideologiia*, no. 5, 1982, 119–26, and no. 6, 1982, 119, 127, and Bruce Parrott, *The Politics of Soviet Defense Spending* (Bloomington, Ind.: Indiana University Press, forthcoming).

9. Bruce Parrott, "Soviet Policy toward the United States: A Fork in the Road?" *SAIS Review* 5, no. 1 (Winter-Spring 1985), 110–11 and passim. (The present chapter draws heavily on the material presented in this article.)

· 10. Leonid Brezhnev, *Leninskim kursom*, VIII (Moscow: Politizdat, 1981), 419; "Rech' General'nogo sekretaria TsK KPSS tovarishcha Iu. V. Andropova," *Kommunist*, no. 9, 1983, 15; "Rech' tovarishcha K. U. Chernenko na vstreche s rabochimi moskovskogo metallurgicheskogo zavoda 'Serp i molot' 29 aprelia 1984 goda," *Kommunist*, no. 7, 1984, 16–17; "Politicheskii doklad Tsentral'nogo Komiteta KPSS XXVII s"ezdu Kommunisticheskoi Partii Sovetskogo Soiuza," *Pravda*, February 27, 1986, 7.

11. "V interesakh povysheniia boevoi gotovnosti," *Kommunist Vooruzhennykh Sil*, no. 14, 1980, 24–30; Nikolai Ogarkov, "Na strazhe mirnogo truda," *Kommunist*, no. 10, 1981, 81–82, and Nikolai Ogarkov, *Vsegda v gotovnosti k zashchite otechestva* (Moscow: Voenizdat, 1982), 20–21, 26–27, 66.

12. "Zashchita sotsializma: opyt istorii i sovremennost'," *Krasnaia zvezda*, May 9, 1984, 2–3.

13. E. Rybkin, "V. I. Lenin, KPSS ob imperializme kak postoiannom istochnike voennoi opasnosti," *Voenno-istoricheskii zhurnal*, no. 4, 1983, 3, 7–9.

14. "Posledovatel'naia i chestnaia politika mira," *Kommunist*, no. 9, 1982, 10. A fuller analysis of this editorial is given in Parrott, *The Politics of Soviet Defense Spending*.

15. A. A. Gromyko, "V. I. Lenin i vneshniaia politika Sovetskogo gosudarstva," *Kommunist*, no. 6, 1983, 11–33.

16. Iu. Molchanov, "Razriadka: istoki i vozmozhnosti," *Kommunist*, no. 13, 1984, 109–10, 112.

17. The 1983 exchange between Rybkin and Gromyko, for example, was clearly related to the question of how to counter the impending deployment of U.S. intermediate-range missiles in Europe. (See Parrott, "Soviet Policy toward the United States," 114–15, and Dan L. Strode and Rebecca V. Strode, "Diplomacy and Defense in Soviet National Security Policy," *International Security* [Fall 1983], 91–116.) The 1984 conflict over the renewal of arms negotiations is discussed further in chap. 5 below.

18. For instance, at the 26th Party Congress Brezhnev found it necessary to tell the party delegates that the idea of peaceful coexistence with the West was "not a groundless utopia." Its fruits, he continued, were real and should be valued highly. (Brezhnev, *Leninskim kursom*, VIII, 469. For Brezhnev's rearguard effort to hold down defense spending, see chap. 4 below.)

19. A. Dobrynin, "Za bez"iadernyi mir, navstrechu XXI veku," *Kommunist*, no. 9, 1986, 24–25.

20. For instance, in the spring of 1980, when it had become clear that the Carter administration had permanently shelved efforts to obtain congressional ratification of the SALT II treaty, one writer claimed that "the Pentagon is drawing up a program to create a new missile defense system, which could signify a violation of the 1972 [ABM] treaty," and another writer said that the United States "may be preparing to renounce" the treaty. (A. Tolkunov, "Militaristskie prigotovleniia," *Pravda*, March 28, 1980, 5, and Iu. Zhukov, "Mezhdunarodnoe obozrenie," *Pravda*, March 30, 1980, 4; Gloria Duffy et al., *Report on Compliance and the Future of Arms Control* [Stanford, Calif.: Stanford University Center for International Security and Arms Control, forthcoming], sec. 5.) Soviet military observers also took note of features of tentative Reagan administration plans, such as the scheme for countering any drastic expansion of Soviet offensive forces by defending MX missile sites with ABM weapons, which would have exceeded the limits established in the ABM treaty. (B. Polynin, "Modernizatsiia raketno-iadernykh sredstv SShA," *Vestnik protivovozdushnoi oborony*, no. 11, 1982, 69.)

21. Meyer, "Soviet Strategic Programmes and the US SDI," 275.

22. A. Dvoretskii, "Kosmos v planakh Pentagona," *Vestnik protivovozdushnoi oborony*, no. 7, 1983, 82.

23. Andropov, *Izbrannye rechi i stat'i*, 250–53.

24. Ibid., 252–53.

25. General-lieutenant I. Rudnev, "Usilenie agressivnosti voennoi doktriny SShA," *Zarubezhnoe voennoe obozrenie*, no. 6, 1985, 7–12.

26. Andropov, *Izbrannye rechi i stat'i*, 250–53.

27. Charles L. Glaser, "Do We Want the Missile Defenses We Can Build?" *International Security* 10, no. 1 (Summer 1985), 47–48.

28. Some Western analysts have suggested that if the Soviets genuinely believe this proposition, they must also value a prospective Soviet BMD system for the advantage it would confer on the USSR if it launched a first strike on the United States. This suggestion, however, assumes that the Soviets believe that a Soviet space-based BMD system would be as effective as a U.S. one and that they are not concerned about possible direct offensive uses of space-based weapons. As argued below, this proposition is implausible.

29. B. I. Bogachev, "Somnitel'nye dovody storonnikov 'zvezdnykh voin,' " *SShA: ekonomika, politika, ideologiia,* no. 5, 1985, 69. From an American perspective, of course, this latter possibility reinforces a deterrent threat intended solely to defend Europe against Soviet conventional attack, but from the Soviet viewpoint it would increase the U.S. temptation to resort to the first use of nuclear arms during a European crisis.

30. Quoted from *Pravda* in FitzGerald, "The Soviet Military on SDI."

31. A. A. Arbatov, *Voenno-strategicheskii paritet i politika SShA* (Moscow: Politicheskaia Literatura, 1984), 235–36, as quoted in FitzGerald, "The Other Side of SDI."

32. "Doklad General'nogo sekretaria TsK KPSS deputata M. S. Gorbacheva," *Kommunist,* no. 17, 1985, 41.

33. R. S. Ovinnikov, "Chto stoit za strategiei 'zvezdnykh voin,' " *SShA: ekonomika, politika, ideologiia,* no. 11, 1985, 24.

34. Philip M. Boffey, "Dark Side of 'Star Wars': System Could Also Attack," *The New York Times,* March 7, 1985, 1.

35. On the general Soviet tendency to assume that Western military innovations will be technologically successful, see Meyer, "Soviet Strategic Programmes and the US SDI," 275.

36. "Doklad General'nogo sekretaria TsK KPSS deputata M. S. Gorbacheva," 35, 38.

37. For a survey of Soviet treatments of Pershing II and ground-launched cruise missiles before their deployment in Europe, see William V. Garner, *Soviet Threat Perceptions of NATO's Eurostrategic Missiles* (Paris: The Atlantic Institute for International Affairs, 1983).

38. Andropov, *Izbrannye rechi i stat'i,* 265; Strobe Talbott, *The Russians and Reagan,* pbk. ed. (New York: Vintage Books, 1984), 124–25.

39. In his press conference at the close of the Reykjavik summit, Gorbachev said he had told President Reagan that the president had made him a "brother-in-arms" in the struggle for SDI. "I so sharply criticize SDI, this gives you the

most persuasive argument that SDI is necessary . . . and you collect applause and financing." In the same statement Gorbachev asserted that SDI did not cause the Soviet Union any anxiety in a military sense. This claim, which was clearly belied by Gorbachev's many previous expressions of alarm about SDI and his statement later in the press conference that SDI could pave the way for dangerous new weapons, was an obvious effort to shore up the Soviet negotiating position. ("Press-konferentsiia M. S. Gorbachev," *Pravda*, October 14, 1986, 2.)

**Chapter 3**

1. This goal crystallized more slowly than the others, as the regime gradually gained a limited understanding that its military programs can provoke formidable Western counterprograms based on superior Western technological capacities. Khrushchev's successors probably decided to enter into sustained arms negotiations with the United States partly because they understood that his exaggerated missile claims (which in an era of tight Soviet secrecy were virtually equivalent, politically, to the construction of real missiles) had been a major cause of the rapid U.S. strategic buildup of the 1960s. In the 1970s the Soviets still underestimated the likelihood that their behavior, military as well as diplomatic, would provoke a campaign for Western rearmament. Nevertheless, their public attempts to dissuade the United States from taking such a path were accompanied by a slowing of the growth of their own defense budget. Within two years of the signing of the SALT I treaty they reduced the rate of growth of their military expenditures, particularly expenditures on strategic weapons. (U.S. Congress, Joint Economic Committee, *Allocation of Resources in the Soviet Union and China—1985* [Washington, D.C.: GPO, 1986], 101.) Moreover, since coming to power Gorbachev has put unprecedented stress on the importance of allaying Western anxieties about Soviet military intentions.

2. On such antinomies in the nuclear age, see especially Robert Jervis, *The Illogic of American Nuclear Strategy* (Ithaca, N.Y.: Cornell University Press, 1984).

3. Soviet policymakers pondering BMD have been compelled, consciously or unconsciously, to make judgments on at least five crucial issues. First, is the current situation of mutual nuclear vulnerability between the superpowers desirable for the sake of crisis stability—that is, to reduce the temptation of either side during a crisis to be the first to launch a nuclear strike? Second, does mutual nuclear vulnerability slow the arms race by reducing the competition between offensive and defensive weapons, and does this deceleration contribute substantially to Soviet security? Third, can the situation of mutual vulnerability be overcome by the progress of technology and the introduction of BMD systems? Fourth, how does the USSR's ability to develop and deploy such weapons compare with the ability of the United States or the West in general? Last, can the development of such technology be significantly affected by East-West diplomatic agreements, or does it have an autonomous momentum that governments, acting collectively, are powerless to check?

4. N. Talensky, "Anti-Missile Systems and Disarmament," *International Affairs*, no. 10 (October 1964), 18, as quoted in Garthoff, "BMD and East-West Relations," 293.

5. See, for instance, G. Gerasimov, "Pervyi udar," *Mezhdunarodnaia zhizn'*, no. 3, 1965, 59.

6. "Vazhnye problemy: Vystuplenie A. N. Kosygina pered angliiskimi i inostrannymi zhurnalistami," *Pravda*, February 11, 1967, 1, 3.

7. Tapes of the speech, for instance, show that Kosygin never stated that the purpose of BMD systems was to save lives. For the details, which strongly suggest that the misquotation of Kosygin's remarks was intentional, see Garthoff, "BMD and East-West Relations," 295–96. On the broader Soviet debate over the wisdom of entering SALT negotiations, see Parrott, *Politics and Technology in the Soviet Union*, 192–202.

8. Johan J. Holst, "Missile Defense: The Soviet Union and the Arms Race," in Johan J. Holst and William Schneider, Jr., eds., *Why ABM? Policy Issues in the Missile Defense Controversy* (New York: Pergamon Press, 1969), 148.

9. Stevens, "The Soviet BMD Program," 190–91, 198–200.

10. *Pravda*, February 11, 1967.

11. Garthoff, "BMD and East-West Relations," 295. Garthoff takes the direction of *Pravda*'s alteration (from Kosygin's actual "not a factor in the arms race" to "not a cause of the arms race") as an implicit acknowledgment by the newspaper that defensive systems do indeed play some role in stimulating the superpower arms competition. The likely meaning of the change, however, strikes me as the opposite. As a rule, Soviet leaders' statements are revised in the media only when their Politburo colleagues disapprove of what they said. Other evidence suggests that at this time Kosygin was pushing for arms-control negotiations with the United States despite resistance within the Politburo (Parrott, *Politics and Technology in the Soviet Union*, 192–94), and the thrust of the other changes in Kosygin's original statement was to deny the need for control of ABM systems. Therefore the purpose of the *Pravda* change on this point was probably to strengthen the denial of a link between ABM and the arms race, which in Kosygin's original remarks had been too tentative.

12. E. Rybkin, "Zakony materialisticheskoi dialektiki i ikh proiavlenie v voennom dele," *Kommunist Vooruzhennykh Sil*, no. 7, 1964, 48, as quoted in McConnell, "Shifts in Soviet Views," 322; Thomas Wolfe, *Soviet Strategy at the Crossroads* (Cambridge, Mass.: Harvard University Press, 1964), 190–93; Deane, *The Role of Strategic Defense in Soviet Strategy*, 25–28, 33–34; FitzGerald, "The Soviet Military on SDI."

13. Parrott, *Politics and Technology in the Soviet Union*, chap. 4. As indicated in an earlier note, Soviet assertions about the USSR's possession of highly effective ABM weapons were probably contrived partly to influence Western military calculations, but they undoubtedly also reflected a real confidence in the ability of the Soviet system to devise such a system in the future.

14. The 1967 treaty obligated the signatories "not to place in orbit around the Earth any objects carrying nuclear weapons or any other kinds of weapons

of mass destruction, install such weapons on celestial bodies, or station such weapons in outer space in any other manner." On the negotiations leading up to the treaty, see Raymond L. Garthoff, "Banning the Bomb in Outer Space," *International Security* 5, no. 3 (Winter 1980–1981), 25–40.

15. Holloway, "The Strategic Defense Initiative and the Soviet Union," 259; V. D. Sokolovskiy, *Soviet Military Strategy*, 3d ed., edited by Harriet Fast Scott (New York: Crane, Russak & Company), 169–70, 258–59.

16. Garthoff, "Mutual Deterrence and Strategic Arms Limitation in Soviet Policy"; Robert L. Arnett, "Soviet Attitudes Towards Nuclear War: Do They Really Think They Can Win?" *Journal of Strategic Studies* 2, no. 2 (September 1979), 172–91.

17. Garthoff, "BMD and East-West Relations," 302.

18. Aleksandr Bovin in Foreign Broadcast Information Service, *Daily Report: Soviet Union*, June 20, 1979, AA6–7, as quoted in Garthoff, "BMD and East-West Relations," 307.

19. O. Grinev and V. Pavlov, "Vazhnyi shag k obuzdaniiu gonki vooruzhenii," *Pravda*, June 22, 1972. According to Garthoff, "BMD and East-West Relations," 307, "Grinev" was the pseudonym of Oleg Grinevsky and "Pavlov" the pseudonym of Victor Pavlovich Karpov, both of whom played an important part in the SALT I negotiations.

20. "Vazhnyi vklad v ukreplenie mira i bezopasnosti," *Pravda*, September 30, 1972, 1–2.

21. Ibid. and *Izvestiia*, August 24, 1972.

22. *Pravda*, September 30, 1972, 2. In 1974 Grechko remarked that from time to time offensive weapons outstripped defense and that reliable defenses against nuclear rockets had "still not been created." The clear implication was that the creation of such systems was desirable and would ultimately be achieved. (Grechko, *Vooruzhennye Sily Sovetskogo gosudarstva*, 1st ed., 174.) The chief of the National Air Defense Forces also adopted an equivocal attitude toward the ABM treaty. (Marshal P. Batitskiy, "The National Air Defense [PVO Strany] Troops," *Voennaia mysl'*, no. 11, 1973, CIA Foreign Press Digest 0049, August 27, 1974, 42–43.)

23. U.S. military representatives also resisted this feature of the treaty. See Gerard Smith, *Doubletalk: The Story of SALT I*, pbk. ed. (New York: University Press of America), 263; Raymond L. Garthoff, *Détente and Confrontation: American-Soviet Relations from Nixon to Reagan* (Washington, D.C.: The Brookings Institution, 1985), 153–54. For a discussion of the treaty limitations themselves, see Abram Chayes, Antonia Handler Chayes, and Eliot Spitzer, "Space Weapons: The Legal Context," *Daedalus* 114, no. 3 (Summer 1985), 198–201.

24. Colonel General of Aviation G. Zimin, "PVO Strany Troops in the Great Patriotic War," *Voennaia mysl'*, no. 5, 1965, CIA Foreign Press Digest 949, November 5, 1966, 116.

25. Holloway, "The Strategic Defense Initiative and the Soviet Union," 259; Army General P. Batitskiy, "Development of the Tactics and Operational Art of the Country's Air Defense (PVO) Troops," *Voennaia mysl'*, no. 10, 1967, CIA Foreign Press Digest 0146/68, October 25, 1968, 28, 36–38.

26. Marshal N. I. Krylov, "Raketnye voiska strategicheskogo naznacheniia," *Voenno-istoricheskii zhurnal*, no. 7, 1967, 20, as quoted in Holloway, "The Strategic Defense Initiative and the Soviet Union," 259.

27. V. Aleksandrov, "The Search for a Solution to the Problems of Antimissile Defense in the US," *Voennaia mysl'*, no. 9, 1965, CIA Foreign Press Digest 952, March 2, 1966, 19–20.

28. I. Zav'yalov, "An Answer to Opponents," *Voennaia mysl'*, no. 10, 1965, CIA Foreign Press Digest, March 25, 1966, 53–54; Major General I. Anureyev, "Determining the Correlation of Forces in Terms of Nuclear Weapons," *Voennaia mysl'*, no. 6, 1967, CIA Foreign Press Digest 0112/68, July 11, 1968, 37–39.

29. Stevens, "The Soviet BMD Program," 200–1.

30. Deane, *The Role of Strategic Defense in Soviet Strategy*, 52–55; Garthoff, "BMD and East-West Relations," 298–99, 313; P. F. Batitskii et al., *Voiska protivovozdushnoi oborony strany: istoricheskii ocherk* (Moscow: Voenizdat, 1968), 362, 370.

31. In 1970, for example, General Zav'yalov remarked, "Nuclear weapons have increasingly confirmed the role of attack as the decisive form of military action and have given rise to the necessity of resolving even defensive tasks by active offensive actions." (Quoted in Strode, "Space-Based Lasers," 116.)

32. Parrott, *Politics and Technology in the Soviet Union*, 181–202; Colonel B. Trushin and Colonel M. Gladkov, "The Economic Foundation of the Military-Technical Policy of a Country," *Voennaia mysl'*, no. 12, 1968, CIA Foreign Press Digest 0102/69, November 3, 1969, 36–38.

33. Parrott, *Politics and Technology in the Soviet Union*, 200–1.

34. Ibid., 194–98, 201–2, 232–36.

35. Grechko, *Vooruzhennye Sily Sovetskogo gosudarstva*, 2d ed., 7, 82–83, 92–93, 100, 190–93; Parrott, *The Politics of Soviet Defense Spending*.

36. *XXV s"ezd KPSS: Stenograficheskii otchet* (Moscow: Politizdat, 1976), I, 26–27, 43–44, 47–49, 64, 78–79.

37. V. M. Bondarenko, *Sovremennaia nauka i razvitie voennogo dela* (Moscow: Voenizdat, 1976), 32, 130–31, 184.

38. Ibid., 131, and McConnell, "Shifts in Soviet Views," 329. Bondarenko singled out a 1964 book for this criticism, but he probably would not have troubled to make such a pointed attack if the objectionable theory had not still enjoyed currency within the Soviet elite.

39. Bondarenko, *Sovremennaia nauka*, 132. The fact that Bondarenko did not attribute this view to Western writers suggests that he was addressing his remarks to a domestic audience. This is consistent with the principal argument of the book, which was clearly intended to persuade domestic decisionmakers of the need to accelerate Soviet military R and D.

40. Ibid.

41. Ibid., 41, 46–49, 62, 64; Parrott, *Politics and Technology in the Soviet Union*, 272.

42. Bondarenko, *Sovremennaia nauka*, 49.

43. According to Bondarenko, the research institutes of the armed forces are charged with performing certain crucial functions that other Soviet scientific establishments cannot perform—particularly the appraisal of the latest results of basic research with respect to possible application for military purposes. In performing this function, according to Bondarenko, the military institutes take into account the "scientific, economic, military, and political (also including the diplomatic) perspectives of such a step. The necessity for such an organization of the question has long been recognized." (Ibid., 41.)

44. The two reviews of the book that appeared in military journals both expressed approval for Bondarenko's call for Soviet military-technical superiority over any potential enemy—and this even after Brezhnev, in a path-breaking political speech, had for the first time explicitly disavowed the goal of Soviet strategic superiority over the West. But the reviewers' responses on specific military points seemed to diverge. The review in the journal of the National Air Defense Forces was unequivocal and exceptionally positive. Noting that some of the book's ideas were controversial, the reviewer pointedly praised its conclusions and generalizations as "substantiated, trustworthy and significant in a practical sense." The book received a rather different evaluation at a "readers' conference" held at the Ground Forces' Military Academy of Antiair Defense—that is, in a sub-branch of the Ground Forces charged with tactical air defense, not strategic air or space defense. While the participants praised some aspects of the book, "a series of speakers" reportedly commented that it should have analyzed more fully "the dialectical interaction of battle means and countermeans." Although this general comment may have been a reference to other types of weapons, it may also have been a veiled allusion to the interaction between ballistic missiles and systems for defending against them. (K. Paiusov, "Nauka i voennoe delo," *Vestnik protivovozdushnoi oborony*, no. 6, 1977, 77–80; A. Aleksandrov, "Nauka i voennoe delo," *Kommunist Vooruzhennykh Sil*, no. 20, 1977; L. I. Brezhnev, *Leninskim kursom*, VI [Moscow: Politizdat, 1978], 293–94.)

45. Marshal of Aviation G. V. Zimin et al., *Razvitie protivovozdushnoi oborony* (Moscow: Voenizdat, 1976), 61–67, 87. At the time this book appeared, Zimin was chief of the Military Academy of the National Air Defense Forces.

46. Ibid., 100. William F. Scott, "The Soviets and Strategic Defense," *Air Force Magazine* 69, no. 3 (March 1986), 42, provides solid evidence that statements about foreign air defense forces are sometimes intended as veiled descriptions of Soviet

programs. In my opinion, however, he exaggerates the frequency of such tacit arguments by analogy, which are exceptions rather than the rule.

47. The writers conveyed this implication in several ways. First, they stressed the likelihood of a major shift of U.S. missile forces from land bases to less vulnerable sea bases, making no mention of the domestic U.S. resistance to such a major restructuring of the strategic triad. Second, they noted that the United States was introducing solid-fuel missiles that could be maintained at high states of readiness for long periods and were therefore less vulnerable to "the strategic means of a retaliatory (sic) attack." Third, the writers cited and did not challenge the alleged opinion of Western leaders that a Western surprise attack could annihilate or significantly weaken an enemy's strategic capability and thereby "guarantee the security of their state." Fourth, in discussing the prospects for a Western attack utilizing simultaneous bomber and missile strikes, the writers omitted any reference to a possible Soviet launch on warning or the customary Soviet assurance that an attack would meet a devastating Soviet retaliatory response. Finally, they stressed that defense against an enemy air or space attack "has great strategic significance for the successful conduct of the struggle by all [branches of] the Armed Forces of the Soviet Union and the member countries of the Warsaw Pact." (Ibid., 71, 87, 91–92, 183–86.)

48. Ibid., 72, 92. In view of later debates about the precise boundaries on research and development established by the ABM treaty, the wording of this statement is significant. The Russian-language version of the treaty obligates both sides "not to create the basis for" a fixed land-based ABM system for protecting their territories and "not to create, not to test, and not to deploy" sea, air, space, or land mobile-based ABM systems or components. (*Pravda*, May 28, 1972, 1.)

49. Zimin et al., *Razvitie protivovozdushnoi oborony*, 102, 105–6, 109, 191–92.

50. Ibid., 92–95.

51. Ibid., 3, 192.

52. P. F. Batitskii, *Voiska protivovozdushnoi oborony strany* (Moscow: Znanie, 1977), 35, 42, 48, 50.

53. In July 1978 the Soviet press identified Batitskii as inspector-general in the Military Inspectorate of the Ministry of Defense—definitely a demotion from his previous position as head of a military service. According to CIA estimates, spending for both the Strategic Rocket Forces and the National Air Defense Forces dropped in absolute terms after 1977. (U.S. Congress, Joint Economic Committee, *Allocation of Resources in the Soviet Union and China—1984* [Washington, D.C.: GPO, 1985], 53–54.)

54. The two U.S. ASAT systems, which were dismantled in the mid-1970s, were based on the Nike Zeus and Thor rockets. See Raymond L. Garthoff, "ASAT Arms Control: Still Possible," *Bulletin of the Atomic Scientists*, August/September 1984, 29–31.

55. U.S. interest in ASAT weapons, which had declined in the early 1970s, was revived largely by the resumption of Soviet testing. The United States committed

itself to a new program of ASAT development in January 1977 and first broached the possibility of Soviet-American ASAT limitation talks in the spring of that year. (Paul B. Stares, *The Militarization of Space: U.S. Policy, 1945–1984* [Ithaca, N. Y.: Cornell University Press, 1985], 157–81.)

56. In 1984 an American authority on Soviet weaponry stated that "the Soviet ASAT interceptor program appears to be a low priority project. After fifteen years of testing different versions of the interceptor system there are no indications that the Soviet Union is trying to create any militarily significant antisatellite capability through this approach." (Meyer, "Space and Soviet Military Planning," 84.)

57. The Soviet system has several serious limitations. It can attack only satellites in low orbits, whereas most strategically significant U.S. satellites are in high orbits. Before attacking, the Soviet ASAT must be placed in an orbit paralleling that of the target, and it relies on active radar to guide it to its prey. Reaching the target thus takes a substantial amount of time, and the ASAT's radar emissions give the target satellite time to maneuver or take other countermeasures. The most recent low-orbit U.S. satellites are equipped to take such measures. (Robert Bowman, *Star Wars: A Defense Expert's Case Against the Strategic Defense Initiative* [Los Angeles, Calif.: Jeremy P. Tarcher, Inc., 1986], 16.) The Soviet effort to develop a more sophisticated ASAT system utilizing a passive infrared homing device that emits no telltale signals has thus far been unsuccessful. All six Soviet tests of such a system have failed. (Ibid.; Thomas K. Longstreth, John E. Pike, and John B. Rhinelander, *The Impact of U.S. and Soviet Ballistic Missile Defense Programs on the ABM Treaty*, 3d ed. [Washington, D.C.: National Campaign to Save the ABM Treaty, 1985], 21.)

58. Donald L. Hafner, "Averting a Brobdingnagian Skeet Shoot: Arms Control Measures for Anti-Satellite Weapons," *International Security* 5, no. 3 (Winter 1980–1981), 41–42; Bowman, *Star Wars*, 16; Strode, "Space-Based Lasers," 110. The post-1982 moratorium is discussed further in chap. 5.

59. A new long-range ABM missile was coupled with a high-acceleration missile. The latter type of missile permits attacks on incoming reentry vehicles in the final phase of their trajectories, when atmospheric sorting can be used to differentiate real warheads from decoys. (Stevens, "The Soviet BMD Program," 209–11.)

60. Ibid., 213–14.

61. Ibid., 215–16.

62. *Soviet Strategic Defense Programs*, 12–16. It also should be noted that among all the components of the Soviet military effort, R and D programs are the most difficult for Western analysts to measure accurately. Some U.S. observers have suggested that this estimate may be too high. (William J. Broad, "Experts Say Soviet Has Conducted Space Tests," *The New York Times*, October 15, 1986.)

63. Holloway, "The Strategic Defense Initiative and the Soviet Union," 262.

64. The Department of Defense estimates that this development could come as early as the late 1990s. The Central Intelligence Agency states that because

of the severe technical requirements, there is only a "low probability" that the Soviets could take this step before 2000. (Office of Technology Assessment, *Ballistic Missile Defense Technologies* [Washington, D.C.: GPO, 1985], 59–61.)

65. Ibid., 217–18; Walter Pincus, "U.S., Soviet at Odds on 'Star Wars,' " *The Washington Post*, September 30, 1985, A1, A4; B. Jeffrey Smith, "U.S. Tops Soviets in Key Weapons Technology," *Science*, May 7, 1986, 1063–64. The USSR, which also lags in materials, signal processing, and propulsion, leads in none of the militarily relevant technologies examined in the annual Department of Defense report. It matches the United States in directed energy and optics, as well as in warheads, aerodynamics, and power sources.

66. G. Trofimenko, "Voennaia strategiia SShA—orudie agressivnoi politiki," *SShA: ekonomika, politika, ideologiia*, no. 1, 1985, 12. See also L. Semeiko, "U opasnoi cherty," *Krasnaia zvezda*, January 23, 1986, 3.

67. V. I. Zamkovoi and M. N. Filatov, *Filosofiia agressii* (Alma-Ata: Kazakhstan, 1981), 230, 270, 276. These passages are cited by FitzGerald, "The Soviet Military on SDI."

68. Zamkovoi and Filatov, *Filosofiia agressii*, 287.

69. At some points the writers claimed that Western ruling circles are "preparing for nuclear war." At other points, however, they emphasized the "weighty fears" restraining Western policymakers from using nuclear weapons, and they argued vigorously that the objective logic of damage limitation through preemptive strikes does not create a subjective disposition on the part of Western decisionmakers to launch a surprise attack on the USSR. (Ibid., 197, 213–14, 303.)

70. N. Ogarkov, "Voennaia nauka i zashchita sotsialisticheskogo otechestva," *Kommunist*, no. 7, 1978, 117.

71. The texts are compared in FitzGerald, "The Soviet Military on SDI." For a discussion of Ogarkov's critique of existing Soviet security policy, see Parrott, *The Politics of Soviet Defense Spending*.

72. Parrott, *The Politics of Soviet Defense Spending*.

73. "Zashchita sotsializma: opyt istorii i sovremennost'," 2–3.

74. I am indebted to Raymond Garthoff for calling this interpretation to my attention. A contrary explanation is that Ogarkov was forced to mute a belief in the future need for a large Soviet BMD not only for reasons of foreign propaganda but because he was in political trouble and the idea remained controversial within the party leadership. The plausibility of this explanation hinges on whether Ogarkov's public change of stance on the relative importance of the Western nuclear and conventional threats was genuine. If his shift of emphasis was a dissimulation intended to parry Chernenko's unusually sanguine views about the current strategic nuclear balance, Ogarkov may privately have been more favorably disposed toward the deployment of a large BMD system than his speeches and writings indicate. On Ogarkov's view toward negotiated limits on SDI, see chap. 5.

75. In 1981 the National Air Defense Forces *(Voiska Protivovozdushnoi Oborony Strany)* were renamed the Air Defense Forces *(Voiska Protivovozdushnoi Oborony)* and about 45 percent of their aircraft were transferred to the Air Forces. (Harriet Fast Scott and William F. Scott, *The Armed Forces of the USSR*, 3d ed. [Boulder, Colo.: Westview Press, 1984], 159–60.) So far as I know, in the 1980s no official of the Air Defense Forces has directly advocated giving that service a role in defending against enemy ballistic missiles. However, in 1982 the commander of the branch stressed that the danger of enemy surprise attack had grown as never before and had made effective air defense "an exceptionally acute problem." As a result, he said, strengthening his service had become a task of "state importance." (Marshal of Aviation A. Koldunov, "Vsemerno ukrepliat' boevoi potentsial Voisk PVO," *Vestnik protivovozdushnoi oborony*, no. 4, 1982, 3–4.) It is probably significant that spokesmen for this service showed an early inclination to emphasize the likelihood that the United States would deploy a large BMD system. One article, pointing out that the United States had continued to spend sizable amounts of money on BMD research and design work, noted that the United States was focusing its attention on a three-tier system. The account glossed over whether the system was already being built but strongly implied that it was. This article went to press in February 1983, a month before President Reagan announced the Strategic Defense Initiative. (S. Gerasimov, "O sisteme protivoraketnoi oborony SShA," *Vestnik protivovozdushnoi oborony*, no. 2, 1983, 78–81.) For a discussion of the economic factors affecting the views of the other services and the party leadership, see chap. 4.

76. Some Western commentators have suggested that the decision to build the installation at Abalakovo was the result of a bureaucratic oversight in which the compatibility of the radar with the ABM treaty was not considered. However, the identity of the industrial personnel responsible for building the installation and the expense of constructing it both indicate that the decision must have been made at a high level by people who were aware of this issue. (Duffy et al., *Report on Compliance and the Future of Arms Control*, sec. 5.)

77. Two U.S. early-warning LPARs, of a type designated as "Pave Paws," were built in Massachusetts and California and became operational in the late 1970s. Two similar LPARs, currently being built in Georgia and Texas, are scheduled to become operational by 1987. The fields covered by the California radar include most of California and a narrow strip of the northern west coast. Each of the four Pave Paws radars has a 240-degree field of coverage. "Initial plans for the deployment of the two new radars resulted in a field of coverage that included almost two-thirds of the continental United States. The final deployment plan apparently will reduce this coverage, but it still includes greater portions of the United States than were covered by the first two radars of this type." (Longstreth, Pike, and Rhinelander, *The Impact of U.S. and Soviet Ballistic Missile Defense Programs on the ABM Treaty*, 40, 71.)

78. This interpretation meshes with other aspects of Soviet treaty-compliance behavior—such as the encryption of missile-test telemetry—that deteriorated markedly in 1979–83 but then began to improve. (Duffy et al., *Report on Compliance and the Future of Arms Control*, sec. 5.)

79. Michael R. Gordon, "CIA Is Skeptical that New Soviet Radar Is Part of an ABM Defense System," *National Journal*, March 9, 1985, 523–26.

80. My discussion of these points draws heavily on Duffy et al., *Report on Compliance and the Future of Arms Control*, sec. 5.

81. Ibid.

82. Ibid.

83. Bjorkman and Zamostny, "Soviet Politics and Strategy Toward the West," 197–98; "Nauchno-tekhnicheskaia revoliutsiia i ee sotsial'nye aspekty," *Kommunist*, no. 12, 1982, 13, 20–21.

**Chapter 4**

1. For a thorough review of the economy's problems and prospects, see Robert Campbell, "The Economy," in Robert F. Byrnes, ed., *After Brezhnev* (Bloomington, Ind.: Indiana University Press, 1983), 68–124.

2. See Richard F. Kaufman, "Causes of the Slowdown in Soviet Defense," along with the commentaries on this article, in *Soviet Economy* 1, no. 1 (January–March 1985), 9–32, and *Allocation of Resources in the Soviet Union and China—1985*, 101.

3. Ogarkov, "Na strazhe mirnogo truda," 81–82, 89–91; Dale R. Herspring, "Marshal Ogarkov and the Structure of Soviet Military Politics: 1980–1985," unpublished paper, Washington, D.C. (Fall 1985), 5.

4. Brezhnev, *Leninskim kursom*, VIII, 469–73; *XXVI s"ezd KPSS*, 63; Konstantin Chernenko, "Leninskaia strategiia rukovodstva," *Kommunist*, no. 13, 1981, 11, 14; Rebecca Strode, "The Soviet Armed Forces: Adaptation to Resource Scarcity," *The Washington Quarterly* (Spring 1986), 59–61; Parrott, *The Politics of Soviet Defense Spending*.

5. G. Sorokin, "Intensifikatsiia i razvitie dvukh podrazdelenii obshchestvennogo proizvodstva," *Planovoe khoziaistvo*, no. 5, 1982, 25–28.

6. *Krasnaia zvezda*, May 9, 1984, 2–3.

7. "Rech' tovarishcha K. U. Chernenko na vstreche s rabochimi moskovskogo metallurgicheskogo zavoda 'Serp i molot' 29 aprelia 1984 goda," 15–17, and "Poleninski zhit', rabotat', borot'sia," 4.

8. These frictions are discussed in a draft article, provisionally entitled "Recent Trends in Soviet Civil-Military Relations," which I am preparing for publication. For other issues that may have helped precipitate Ogarkov's demotion, see chap. 5.

9. Parrott, *Politics and Technology in the Soviet Union*, 252–53, 272.

10. *XXVI s"ezd KPSS*, 43–44, 62; Parrott, *Politics and Technology in the Soviet Union*, 406n.

11. V. Ermanchenkov, "Deiatel'nost' KPSS po ukrepleniiu oboronosposob-nosti strany na sovremennom etape," *Kommunist Vooruzhennykh Sil*, no. 15, 1980, 68; Ogarkov, *Vsegda v gotovnosti k zashchite otechestva*, 30.

12. *Pravda*, October 28, 1982, 1; Parrott, *The Politics of Soviet Defense Spending*.

13. V. Bondarenko, "Edinaia nauchno-tekhnicheskaia politika KPSS," *Kommunist Vooruzhennykh Sil*, no. 19, 1984, 14. (This article was reprinted verbatim in the journal of the Air Defense Forces.) See also Marshal V. Petrov, "Na strazhe mirnogo truda sovetskogo naroda," *Kommunist*, no. 3, 1984, 84–85.

14. V. Kornienko, "Dlia blaga sovetskogo cheloveka," *Kommunist Vooruzhennykh Sil*, no. 2, 1980, 22–26; Iu. Vlas'evich, "Ekonomicheskaia strategiia partii," *Kommunist Vooruzhennykh Sil*, no. 4, 1980, 18–22, 25; S. Bartenev, "Ekonomika i voennaia moshch'," *Kommunist Vooruzhennykh Sil*, no. 14, 1980, 66, 70–71; A. Dmitriev, "Boevoi potentsial i boevaia gotovnost' Sovetskikh Vooruzhennykh Sil," *Kommunist Vooruzhennykh Sil*, no. 3, 1983, 17; Parrott, *The Politics of Soviet Defense Spending*.

15. Jan Vanous and Bryan Roberts, "Time to Choose Between Tanks and Tractors: Why Gorbachev Must Come to the Negotiating Table or Face a Collapse of His Ambitious Modernization Program," *PlanEcon Report: Developments in the Economies of the Soviet Union and Eastern Europe* II, nos. 25–26, 1–16.

16. "Doklad General'nogo sekretaria TsK KPSS M. S. Gorbacheva," *Pravda*, April 24, 1985, 1.

17. Dale R. Herspring, "The Soviet Military in the Aftermath of the 27th Party Congress," *Orbis* 30, no. 2 (Summer 1986), 311; Robert Campbell, "Resource Stringency and the Civilian-Military Resource Allocation," unpublished paper, 25–26. I am grateful to Professor Campbell for permission to read and cite his paper.

18. Campbell, "Resource Stringency and the Civilian-Military Resource Allocation," 23.

19. "Krepit' oboronu strany," *Kommunist Vooruzhennykh Sil*, no. 2, 1986, 28–30; also A. Dmitriev, "Prochnyi splav," *Krasnaia zvezda*, June 27, 1986, 2–3.

20. In the sequence of factors said to contribute to the might of the armed forces, equipment and technology were moved from last to second place. However, a proposal to spell out more fully the material components of military might, such as equipment and manpower, was not accepted. ("Programma Kommunisticheskoi partii Sovetskogo Soiuza (novaia redaktsiia)," *Kommunist*, no. 16, 1985, 35; *XXVII s"ezd KPSS: stenograficheskii otchet* (Moscow: Politizdat, 1986), I, 595–96; "Rech' tovarishcha Gorbacheva M. S. na vstreche s trudiashchimisia goroda Tol'iatti," *Pravda*, April 9, 1986, 2. I am grateful to Timothy Colton and Ellen Jones for bringing Gorbachev's speech and the change in the formula to my attention.

21. Gary Lee, "Soviet Marshal Issues Call for High-Technology Arms," *The Washington Post*, October 28, 1986, A21. Initial Western reports indicate that

Ogarkov's article was excerpted from a pamphlet published in 1985, but that it omitted the pamphlet's pointed warning about the potentially dangerous implications of "mistakes" in Soviet defense policy.

22. Jerry Hough, "Soviet Interpretation and Response," in *Arms Control and the Strategic Defense Initiative: Three Perspectives*, (Muscatine, Iowa: The Stanley Foundation, Occasional Paper 36, October 1985), 7–12.

23. In my opinion, total resource demands will increase even though the pursuit of SDI will probably slow U.S. progress in other types of weaponry, because the Soviets already perceive a U.S. challenge in these other military realms. On the possibility that a Soviet SDI program might obstruct economic reform, see David Holloway, "State of the Union," *New York Review of Books* 33, no. 10 (June 12, 1986), 20.

24. In 1983, less than a month before President Reagan announced SDI, the USSR Academy of Sciences took the important step of establishing a new Department of Informatics, Computer Technology, and Automation. The department, whose creation was reportedly promoted by the party Central Committee, was headed by E.P. Velikhov, a scientist active in research on pulsed power and other subjects relevant to space defense. The motives for establishing the department included a growing awareness of the strategic implications of computer technology and concern about the more stringent limitations being imposed on Soviet access to Western computer know-how. (Simon Kassel, *A New Force in the Soviet Computer Industry: The Reorganization of the USSR Academy of Sciences in the Computer Field*, N–2486–ARPA [Santa Monica, Calif.: Rand Corporation, 1986]; *Vestnik Akademii nauk SSSR*, no. 6, 1983, 11–12, 40–41.) In 1986 the academy established another new unit, the Division of Problems of Machinebuilding, Mechanics, and Control Processes, which was apparently set up partly to contribute to military programs. (Campbell, "Resource Stringency and the Civilian-Military Resource Allocation," 25.)

25. *Allocation of Resources in the Soviet Union and China—1985*, 53, 115; Campbell, "Resource Stringency and the Civilian-Military Resource Allocation," 15–16. For a valuable recent overview of Soviet computer technology, see S. E. Goodman, "Technology Transfer and the Development of the Soviet Computer Industry," in Bruce Parrott, ed., *Trade, Technology, and Soviet-American Relations* (Bloomington, Ind.: Indiana University Press, 1985), 117–40. For a survey of the limitations of Soviet software development, see W. K. McHenry, P. Wolcott, and S. E. Goodman, "Soviet Large-Scale Software Development Management," unpublished paper, March 1986.

26. *Allocation of Resources in the Soviet Union and China—1985*, 9, 55–57, 118.

27. In the USSR, for instance, such controversies were especially pronounced in the early 1960s, when Khrushchev assigned a greater strategic role to nuclear missiles and tried to cut the overall defense budget. The resulting doctrinal disputes were not purely interservice rivalries, but they were certainly strengthened by such rivalries. See Wolfe, *Soviet Strategy at the Crossroads*.

28. For instance, V.V. Lipaev and A.I. Potapov, "Programmnoe obespechenie dlia EVM voennogo naznacheniia," *SShA: ekonomika, politika, ideologiia*, no. 4, 1985,

113–18. See also William Odom, "Soviet Force Posture: Dilemmas and Decisions," *Problems of Communism* 34, no. 4 (July–August 1985), 8–11.

29. McConnell, *Analyzing the Soviet Press*, 2–3, 5–6, 10–11. The quotation is from Colonel S. Bartenev, "Vroven' s progressom ekonomiki, nauki, tekhniki," *Kommunist Vooruzhennykh Sil*, no. 5, 1983, 21.

30. The conflicting claims of the Strategic Rocket Forces and National Air Defense Forces were examined above. See also Garthoff, "BMD and East-West Relations," 298–99.

31. For instance, compare V. A. Aleksandrov, "Evoliutsiia amerikanskikh vzgliadov na vozmozhnyi kharakter voin," *Voenno-istoricheskii zhurnal*, no. 6, 1985, 62, with P. A. Zhilin, "Razvitie leninskogo ucheniia o zashchite sotsialisticheskogo Otechestva v materialakh XXVII s"ezda KPSS," *Voenno-istoricheskii zhurnal*, no. 7, 1986, 5.

## Chapter 5

1. For the text of the draft treaty, see U.S. Congress, Office of Technology Assessment, *Anti-Satellite Weapons, Countermeasures, and Arms Control* (Washington, D.C.: GPO, 1985), 145–46.

2. "Priem Iu. V. Andropovym amerikanskikh senatorov," *SShA: ekonomika, politika, ideologiia*, no. 10, 1983, 6.

3. For the text of the 1981 draft, see Foreign Broadcast Information Service, *Daily Report: Soviet Union*, August 12, 1981, AA16–18. On Brezhnev's call for such limitations, see chap. 4 above.

4. The administration also refused to participate in multilateral negotiations over the 1983 draft. (*Anti-Satellite Weapons, Countermeasures, and Arms Control*, 96.) The administration announced its agreement to participate in bilateral INF talks late in September 1981; it agreed to strategic arms reduction (START) negotiations in May 1982.

5. Horelick and Warner, "U.S.-Soviet Nuclear Arms Control," 230.

6. The first of these incidents occurred in February. Chernenko's second statement omitting the precondition was made on September 2 and corrected by the Foreign Ministry on September 3. (Elizabeth Teague, "Factions in the Kremlin," *Radio Liberty Research Bulletin*, no. 39, 1984, 4–5.)

7. "Otvety K. U. Chernenko na voprosy gazety 'Pravdy,' " *Kommunist*, no. 13, 1984, 6–8; Iu. Molchanov, "Razriadka: istoki i vozmozhnosti," 109–10, 112. The fact that these anti-détente skeptics were described as "well-intentioned" and were not identified makes it virtually certain that they were members of Soviet rather than Western ruling circles.

8. "Rech' tovarishcha G. V. Romanova," *Pravda*, September 8, 1984, 4.

9. "Rech' tovarishcha M. S. Gorbacheva," *Pravda*, September 9, 1984, 4.

10. TASS issued Chernenko's new bid on September 5. (Teague, "Factions in the Kremlin.")

11. "Soviet Accepts Bid to Have Gromyko Meet with Reagan," *The New York Times*, September 11, 1984, A1, A9.

12. Don Oberdorfer, "Gromyko in U.N. Speech Assails Reagan Policies," *The Washington Post*, September 28, 1984, A1.

13. Nikolai Ogarkov, "Nemerknushchaia slava sovetskogo oruzhiia," *Kommunist Vooruzhennykh Sil*, no. 21, 1984, 16–26; *Facts on File*, 1984, 800. For an analysis of the changes in Ogarkov's position on the issues, see Parrott, *The Politics of Soviet Defense Spending*.

14. *The New York Times*, November 23, 1984, as cited by Horelick and Warner, "U.S.-Soviet Nuclear Arms Control," 230; Celestine Bohlen, "Soviet Asks Broadened Arms Talks," *The Washington Post*, November 27, 1984, A1.

15. The terms stated that issues touching strategic arms, intermediate-range arms, and space arms were to be "considered and resolved in their interrelationship," and that the aim concerning space weapons was to prevent "an arms race in space." These elastic formulas left open the question of whether there would be trade-offs between the three types of weapons and whether space weapons might be introduced on an agreed basis. (Horelick and Warner, "U.S.-Soviet Nuclear Arms Control," 230–31.)

16. S. Akhromeev, "Dogovor po PRO—pregrada na puti gonki strategicheskikh vooruzhenii," *Pravda*, June 14, 1985, 4. Akhromeev cautioned that before World War II a "definite gap" had opened up between Soviet military-theoretical thought and the practical preparation of the armed forces. Once the war began, he said, *"the problem of conducting defense on a strategic scale confronted the Soviet government as extremely urgent and especially important."* Later he observed that the war had forced "all," including the supreme commander, to revise their military ideas. (S. Akhromeev, "Prevoskhodstvo sovetskoi voennoi nauki i sovetskogo voennogo iskusstva—odin iz vazhneishikh faktorov pobedy v Velikoi Otechestvennoi voine," *Kommunist*, no. 3, 1985, 51, 54. Emphasis in the original.) The contemporary lessons of the 1930s and World War II had been a major point of contention between Ogarkov and his critics. (Parrott, *The Politics of Soviet Defense Spending*.)

17. N. V. Ogarkov, *Istoriia uchit bditel'nosti* (Moscow: Voenizdat, 1985), 27–28, 32–33, 36. (The work was sent to the compositor in February and signed for printing in April.)

18. "Doklad General'nogo sekretaria TsK KPSS M. S. Gorbacheva," *Pravda*, April 24, 1985, 2; Dusko Doder, "Gorbachev Says Talks Could Collapse," *The Washington Post*, June 25, 1985, A32.

19. See chap. 4.

114    The Soviet Union and Ballistic Missile Defense

20. According to one Western tally, in recent years the USSR has set off approximately twenty-four nuclear explosions annually; an average of about fourteen of these have been weapons tests. (Michael R. Gordon, "Soviet Reported Acting to Begin New Atom Tests," *The New York Times*, March 18, 1986, A1, A4.)

21. Horelick and Warner, "U.S.-Soviet Nuclear Arms Control," 232–33, 245–46.

22. "Text of Joint U.S.-Soviet Statement," *The Washington Post*, November 22, 1985, A25.

23. "Doklad General'nogo sekretaria TsK KPSS deputata M. S. Gorbacheva," *Kommunist*, no. 17, 1985, 35–43.

24. "Rech' deputata V. V. Shcherbitskogo," *Izvestiia*, November 28, 1985, 3.

25. "U.S. Not Sure if Soviet Links Missile Accord to 'Star Wars,' " *The New York Times*, February 6, 1986, A10.

26. "Rech' deputata S. F. Akhromeeva," *Izvestiia*, November 28, 1985, 4.

27. "Vysokaia otvetstvennost', novatorskii podkhod," *Krasnaia zvezda*, December 31, 1985.

28. V. Pustov, "Zheneva: do i posle," *Krasnaia zvezda*, November 24, 1985, 3. This commentary was published before Gorbachev delivered his own report on the Geneva meeting.

29. Fedor Burlatskii in *Literaturnaia gazeta*, November 27, 1985, as quoted in Bohdan Nahaylo, "A Difficult Week Ahead for Eduard Shevardnadze," *Radio Liberty Research Bulletin*, RL 353/86, no. 39 (September 24, 1986), 3. Burlatskii has a long history of championing relatively moderate policies toward the United States.

30. For example, one military editorial proclaimed that the summit had done "major work" and that the joint statement that nuclear war was impermissible and that neither side would pursue military superiority was "fundamentally important." The summit, it said, had created the conditions for an improvement in the international environment and for a return to détente. ("Otvetstvennost' za sud'bu mira," *Krasnaia zvezda*, November 26, 1985, 1.)

31. "V interesakh mira i bezopasnosti narodov," *Kommunist Vooruzhennykh Sil*, no. 1, 1986, 10.

32. Ibid., 9–14.

33. The package treated the INF-SDI linkage ambiguously. It stated that an agreement to cut superpower weapons capable of reaching the other superpower—which obviously included not only strategic forces but U.S. INF missiles in Europe—was impossible without curbs on SDI, but the separate passage proposing to liquidate all INF missiles in Europe mentioned no such precondition.

("Zaiavlenie General'nogo sekretaria TsK KPSS M. S. Gorbacheva," *Izvestiia*, January 16, 1986, 1; *The New York Times*, February 8, 1986.)

34. *The New York Times*, May 31, 1986; June 14, 1986; and June 17, 1986.

35. The X-ray laser is one SDI technology that would clearly be blocked by a comprehensive nuclear test ban.

36. Gorbachev addressed a large meeting of Soviet diplomatic personnel in the second half of May, with Dobrynin and other foreign-policy overseers in attendance, and extensive staff changes at the Ministry of Foreign Affairs ensued. The text of Gorbachev's speech has not been published. (Alexander Rahr, "Winds of Change Hit Foreign Ministry," *Radio Liberty Research Bulletin*, RL 274/86, no. 30 (July 23, 1986), 1–10; Serge Schmemann, "Gorbachev Convenes Aides and Gives a Critique of Foreign Policy," *The New York Times*, May 24, 1986, 4.)

37. The United States had staged its last nuclear test in December 1985 and was scheduled to conduct a new test at the end of March.

38. Gordon, "Soviet Reported Acting to Begin New Atom Tests," A1, A4.

39. Serge Schmemann, "Gorbachev Seeks to Talk to Reagan on Atom Test Ban," *The New York Times*, March 30, 1986, 1, 16.

40. William J. Broad, "U.S. Researchers Foresee Big Rise in Nuclear Tests," *The New York Times*, April 21, 1986, A1, A7; Philip Taubman, "Yearlong Soviet Atom-Test Halt Expires," *The New York Times*, August 7, 1986.

41. One other possible explanation for the delay is that it was intended to increase pressure on the Reagan administration to accept the idea of a U.S. moratorium. While this explanation cannot be ruled out entirely, it does not account for the evidence of internal Soviet friction over the May renewal.

42. Herspring, "The Soviet Military in the Aftermath of the 27th Party Congress."

43. Television interview with Aleksandr Bovin, quoted in Bohdan Nahaylo, "The Soviet Military and the Kremlin's Moratorium on Nuclear Tests," *Radio Liberty Research Bulletin*, RL 381/86, no. 42 (October 15, 1986), 3.

44. Dobrynin, "Za bez"iadernyi mir, navstrechu XXI veku," 25. This issue of the journal was sent to the compositor between May 22 and June 9 and signed for printing on June 11.

45. In 1985 the announcement that the moratorium would start on August 6 was made in the final days of July.

46. Chervov also stated that such differences were "an internal matter for us." (*Sovetskaia Rossiia*, August 23, 1986, as quoted in Nahaylo, "The Soviet Military and the Kremlin's Moratorium on Nuclear Tests," 5.)

47. By contrast, Akhromeev had made a clear statement of support to a Western interviewer in mid-April. See Philip Taubman, "Soviet Says Its Nuclear Ban Is Militarily Beneficial to U.S.," *The New York Times*, August 26, 1986, A4; *The Guardian*, April 15, 1986; and *Moscow Radio*, August 25, 1986, in *FBIS Daily Report: Soviet Union*, August 26, 1986, A4.

48. Dobrynin, "Za bez"iadernyi mir, navstrechu XXI veku," 19. Western news reports indicate that the new Soviet offers in Geneva (1) formalized the USSR's January proposal to equalize INF missiles and ultimately eliminate them; (2) dropped the earlier Soviet demand that U.S. forward-based forces be treated as "strategic" weapons; and (3) allowed for deployment of long-range submarine-launched cruise missiles, which the United States had sought. (Michael R. Gordon, "Moscow Presents Pact to Eliminate Missiles in Europe," *The New York Times*, May 16, 1986, A1, A6; Walter Pincus and Don Oberdorfer, "Swift Response Urged to Soviet Arms Offer," *The Washington Post*, June 14, 1986, A20; Michael R. Gordon, "U.S. Arms Officials Finding Problems in Offer by Soviet," *The New York Times*, June 17, 1986, A1, A6.)

49. "Rech' deputata S. F. Akhromeeva."

50. Dobrynin, "Za bez"iadernyi mir, navstrechu XXI veku," 26.

51. Ibid., 23.

52. Quoted in Gary Lee, "Talks Are a Gamble for Soviet Leader," *The Washington Post*, October 1, 1986, A1, A24.

53. *Sovetskaia Rossiia*, October 7, 1986, 3, translated in *FBIS Daily Report: Soviet Union*, October 8, 1986, DD4–5.

54. "Press-konferentsiia M. S. Gorbacheva," *Pravda*, October 14, 1986, 2.

55. Ibid.

56. Falin, chief of the Novosti Press Agency, made this remark in an interview published in the Vienna *Kurier*, October 30, 1986, reprinted in *FBIS Daily Report: Soviet Union*, October 31, 1986, R4–5. (I am grateful to Dawn Mann for calling this item to my attention.) Although in theory such a statement might be explained as a Soviet negotiating tactic designed to foster a Western impression of Soviet hard-liners who will prevent soft-liners from making further concessions, this explanation suffers from two defects. First, it goes against the traditional Soviet emphasis on showing complete internal solidarity in negotiations with other states. Second, it fails to explain why other Soviet spokesmen have tried so hard in recent months to dispel Western impressions of internal Soviet disagreements over strategy toward the United States.

57. *Sovetskaia Rossiia*, October 29, 1986, 5, translated in *FBIS Daily Report: Soviet Union*, November 4, 1986, AA7–8.

58. Thus, for instance, Victor Karpov, the chief Soviet negotiator for the Geneva talks, reportedly said that the INF and nuclear test ban issues could be

negotiated separately from the missile defense issue. Shortly afterward, a Foreign Ministry press spokesman said the Soviet proposals at Reykjavik were a single package. (Serge Schmemann, "Russian Critical," *The New York Times*, October 15, 1986, A1, A13; Serge Schmemann, "Soviet Trying to Explain Arms Linkage Issue," *The New York Times*, October 17, 1986.)

59. "Press-konferentsiia M. S. Gorbacheva," 1, 2.

60. See, for example, the statement by Egor Ligachev translated in *FBIS Daily Report: Soviet Union*, November 7, 1986, R2, and the statement of Eduard Shevardnadze cited in Philip Taubman, "Shevardnadze Specifies Limit on 'Star Wars' Test," *The New York Times*, November 11, 1986, A8.

61. On pressures from American conservatives for immediate new ABM deployments, see Lou Cannon and Sidney Blumenthal, "Reagan SDI Talk Leaves Conservatives Uneasy," *The Washington Post*, August 7, 1986. On the SDI timetable, see Longstreth, Pike, and Rhinelander, *The Impact of U.S. and Soviet Ballistic Missile Defense Programs on the ABM Treaty*, 15, 18.

62. Karen DeYoung, "Soviet Union Loses Ground in Vienna," *The Washington Post*, November 7, 1986, A33.

63. Marshal Akhromeev, for example, has emphasized that a refusal to limit SDI will rule out the limitation as well as the actual reduction of strategic weapons and that "any sort of effort to limit strategic offensive weapons in conditions of the creation of space-strike weapons becomes hopeless." In view of the strategic logic of this position it is reasonable to assume that Akhromeev is voicing a real military opinion rather than mere propaganda. (S. Akhromeev, "Dogovor po PRO—pregrada na puti gonki strategicheskikh vooruzhenni," 4.)

64. Thus, for example, one senior Soviet arms-control official has remarked that "the main destabilizing part of SDI is the space ABM system and its components." (TASS, October 17, 1986, in *FBIS Daily Report: Soviet Union*, October 21, 1986, AA14.)

65. See chap. 6.

66. David E. Sanger, "Many Hesitant to Share 'Star Wars,' " *The New York Times*, November 30, 1985, 3.

67. S. Akhromeev, "Dogovor po PRO—pregrada na puti gonki strategicheskikh vooruzhenii," 4. I am indebted to Stanley Kober for calling this passage to my attention and for allowing me to read his unpublished article, "Moscow's Real Views of the ABM Treaty," on this subject.

68. After the November 1985 Geneva summit Gorbachev assured the Supreme Soviet that if the United States persisted in its plans for the militarization of space, "We will find an answer, as has happened many times in the past." The answer, he said, would be "a real answer, sufficiently quick and, perhaps, less expensive" than SDI. (Quoted by A. Krukhmalev in *KVS*, no. 1, 1986, 22–23.) The accent on quickness and cheapness seems to indicate a preference for an offensive

rather than a BMD response. The statement about needless expenditures is quoted in Philip Taubman, "Gorbachev Says Soviet Test Halt Is Again Extended," *The New York Times*, August 19, 1986, A1, A13. His statement promising an asymmetrical response is contained in "Press-konferentsiia M. S. Gorbacheva," 2.

69. Dobrynin, "Za bez"iadernyi mir, navstrechu XXI veku," 22. Although Dobrynin cited a statement by Gorbachev for authority, his phrasing departed slightly from the general secretary's. Whereas Gorbachev stated that the Soviet response would be "sufficiently quick," Dobrynin said that it would "perhaps" be actualized more quickly than SDI; and whereas Gorbachev said that the answer would "perhaps" be less expensive, Dobrynin omitted this qualifier.

70. In the early 1980s one element of the internal debate over the Soviet defense budget concerned whether higher defense spending would harm the economy and whether the U.S. buildup was a "provocation" meant to achieve this end. (Parrott, *The Politics of Soviet Defense Spending*.) In 1985 one of the exponents of this point of view, a deputy director of the Institute of the USA and Canada, gave a lengthy analysis of the threatening aspects of SDI and promised that the USSR would decisively resist U.S. efforts to obtain "unilateral advantages" through such a system. He immediately added the caveat, however, that "the Soviet Union, naturally, has the possibility to choose those measures that best answer the interests of its defense capacity, taking as a point of departure the general tasks of socioeconomic development of the country." (A. Kokoshin in *Pravda*, June 14, 1985, 4.) In the same issue of *Pravda* in which Kokoshin's article appeared, Marshal Akhromeev promised that the USSR would counter further development of U.S. missile defenses with both offensive and defensive measures of its own.

71. Don Oberdorfer, "Military Response Planned to 'Star Wars,' Soviet Says," *The Washington Post*, March 8, 1985, A1.

72. Akhromeev stated that if the United States creates a large-scale space-based BMD system, the USSR "will be compelled...to expand its strategic offensive forces, augmenting them with means of defense." (*Pravda*, June 14, 1985, 4; see also "Soviet Says Its Nuclear Ban Is Militarily Beneficial to U.S.," 4.)

73. B. M. Shabanov in *Krasnaia zvezda*, November 14, 1985, 3.

74. Holloway, "The Strategic Defense Initiative and the Soviet Union," 269.

75. Robert M. Gates and Lawrence K. Gershwin, "Soviet Strategic Force Developments: Testimony before a Joint Session of the Subcommittee on Strategic and Theater Nuclear Forces of the Senate Armed Services Committee and the Defense Subcommittee of the Senate Committee on Appropriations, June 26, 1985," (photocopy) 1–4.

76. According to the CIA, the deployment of 21,000 warheads "would require a substantially greater commitment of resources" but "is not a maximum [Soviet] effort." (Gates and Gershwin, "Soviet Strategic Force Developments," 4.)

77. Michael Gordon, "Treaty is Said to Keep Soviet from Outdeploying U.S. in Weapons," *The New York Times*, March 31, 1986, A4; interview with Dr. Edward Warner III, November 18, 1986.

78. The limits of cost-exchange calculations in shaping the decisions of either superpower are pointed out by Charles L. Glaser, "Do We Want the Missile Defenses We Can Build?" 37–39.

79. John M. Collins, *U.S.-Soviet Military Balance 1980–1985* (Washington, D.C.: Pergamon-Brassey's, 1985), 55; Gates and Gershwin, "Soviet Strategic Force Developments," 3–4.

## Chapter 6

1. Michael R. Gordon, "Soviet Building 2 Big Radars," *The New York Times*, August 16, 1986. For a discussion of Soviet compliance with arms-control agreements generally, see James A. Schear, "Arms Control Treaty Compliance: Buildup to a Breakdown?" *International Security* 10, no. 2 (Fall 1985), 141–82. For an analysis that raises serious questions about the genuineness of the Reagan administration's professed desire to resolve the issue of Soviet compliance with the ABM treaty, see Michael Krepon, "How Reagan Is Killing a Quiet Forum for Arms Talks," *The Washington Post*, August 31, 1986, D1, D2.

2. Keith B. Payne, "The Soviet Union and Strategic Defense: The Failure and Future of Arms Control," *Orbis*, 29, no. 4 (Winter 1986), 683–89.

3. Pipes, "Why the Soviet Union Thinks It Could Fight and Win a Nuclear War," 21–34.

4. See, in this connection, Mary C. FitzGerald, "Marshal Ogarkov on the Modern Theater Operation," *Naval War College Review*, 39, no. 4 (Autumn 1986), 6–25, and L. Semeiko, "U opasnoi cherty," *Krasnaia zvezda*, January 23, 1986, 3.

5. Each side would retain an ability to detect an impending attack through radars based on its own territory, particularly over-the-horizon radars. However, these radars might themselves become vulnerable to direct attacks from space-based weapons. (On the Soviet early-warning network, see *Soviet Military Power 1986* [Washington, D.C.: GPO, 1986], 43–45.)

6. For technical and geographic reasons, the United States currently depends more heavily on satellites for general reconnaissance and military functions than does the USSR; moreover, a smaller portion of the U.S. satellite network is currently vulnerable to existing ASAT weapons. On the other hand, the Soviet Union has a much greater capacity to put new satellites into orbit. Consequently, if sophisticated ASAT systems were deployed by both sides and war did break out between them, the United States would be less able than the USSR to replace the satellites it had lost to enemy ASAT attacks. If the war was protracted, this could be a serious military disadvantage. (Meyer, "Anti-satellite Weapons and Arms Control: Incentives and Disincentives from the Soviet and American Perspectives," 474–78.)

7. This threat will certainly apply to space assets in low-earth orbits but not necessarily to assets in high-earth orbits or geosynchronous orbits. In order to destroy enemy missiles rising through the atmosphere, BMD weapons must be stationed in low-earth orbits. Because the striking power of these weapons will

diminish sharply with increased distance from the target, they will be able to destroy other weapons and satellites in low-earth orbits but not objects in higher orbits. (Ashton B. Carter, "Satellites and Anti-Satellites: The Limits of the Possible," *International Security* 10, no. 4 [Spring 1986], 96.)

8. This is another variant of the concept of an "offensive breakout" in which one side's offenses suddenly acquire an asymmetrical ability to penetrate the other side's defenses. (Charles L. Glaser, "The Transition to Highly Effective Strategic Defenses," paper prepared for the conference on "Strategic Defense and Soviet-American Relations," Woodrow Wilson International Center for Scholars, Washington, D.C., March 10–11, 1986, 22–25.) As Glaser notes, the introduction of highly effective BMD systems by both sides would increase the danger of such a breakout through rapid offensive deployments or improvements. It would also increase the danger of a breakout through surprise attack on the other side's defenses.

9. For example, assistant secretary of defense Richard Perle answered a journalist's question about Soviet fears of SDI as follows: "I think they've come to some conclusions about the potential for strategic defense, and conceivably, because they weigh great emphasis on this [sic], they have also discovered the potential for offensive uses of space that we haven't yet discovered. But they seem concerned that we might somehow, in the course of the SDI program, stumble upon offensive technologies, and they're trying to stop that. And my guess is that they have already stumbled upon such technologies." ("Briefing by Assistant Secretary of Defense Richard Perle, Tuesday, October 14, 1986, 11:30 A.M. EDT," Federal News Service, 3-1 [photocopy].) This constitutes a clear acknowledgment that space-based BMD may yield offensive weapons, although it does not state that this is the purpose of the SDI program.

10. Robert English, "Offensive Space Weapons," unpublished paper, November 1986, 2, 5. I am grateful to Mr. English for allowing me to read and cite this paper. At present there are fewer than 100 critical command, control, and communications targets in the United States. (Charles L. Glaser, "Do We Want the Missile Defenses We Can Build?" 32.) Some of these targets, of course, are hardened against attack, but others are not, and some, such as LPARs, probably cannot be protected.

11. Glaser, "The Transition to Highly Effective Strategic Defenses," 22–25.

12. While proclaiming that the USSR did not fear SDI, Gorbachev remarked that SDI could pave the way for dangerous new types of weapons. He added that "we also can say that on the basis of our competence *(kompetentno)*." ("Press-konferentsiia M. S. Gorbacheva," 2.)

13. One of the central problems of effective space-based BMD is to create an unprecedented information-processing capacity to identify and track large numbers of rapidly moving enemy missiles and destroy them very quickly. By contrast, terrestrial targets would be easier to target and could be subjected to a more sustained attack.

14. An ATBM limit would be of special benefit to the United States because the acquisition of such systems would offer the USSR an asymmetrical, albeit

marginal, BMD advantage. Soviet ATBMs would possess a marginal BMD potential against SLBMs because they would be deployed opposite enemy tactical missiles near the Soviet homeland; U.S. ATBMs, by contrast, would be deployed against Soviet tactical missiles overseas, far from the United States. It is worth noting that ATBMs were originally omitted from the coverage of the ABM treaty partly because the United States was interested in developing its own ATBMs and did not want the program to be impeded. (Stevens, "The Soviet BMD Program," 208. See also Garthoff, "BMD and East-West Relations," 320–21.)

15. This theme is developed in Jervis, *The Illogic of American Nuclear Strategy,* 37–40.

Other Publications of
The Johns Hopkins University
Foreign Policy Institute

## FPI CASE STUDIES

*The Panama Canal Negotiations*, Wm. Mark Habeeb and I. William Zartman (1986), $3.50
*The New GATT Trade Round*, Charles Pearson and Nils Johnson (1986), $3.50

## FPI POLICY STUDY GROUPS

*Trade Policy: Three Issues*, Isaiah Frank, ed. (1986), $5.00
*U.S.-Soviet Relations*, Simon Serfaty, ed. (1985), $5.00

## FPI POLICY BRIEFS

*Arms Control: A Skeptical Appraisal and a Modest Proposal*, Robert E. Osgood, April 1986, $3.95
*Thinking About SDI*, Stephen J. Hadley, March 1986, $3.95
*The French Fifth Republic: Steadfast and Changing*, Simon Serfaty, February 1986, $3.95
*Mexico in Crisis: The Parameters of Accommodation*, Bruce Michael Bagley, January 1986, $3.95
*The Middle East: Timing and Process*, I. William Zartman, January 1986, $3.95
*Summit Diplomacy in East-West Relations*, Charles H. Fairbanks, Jr., October 1985, $3.95
*The Gandhi Visit: Expectations and Realities of the U.S.-Indian Relationship*, Thomas Perry Thornton, May 1985 (out of print)
*Lebanon: Whose Failure?* Barry Rubin, May 1985 (out of print)
*Living with the Summits: From Rambouillet to Bonn*, Simon Serfaty and Michael M. Harrison, April 1985 (out of print)

## SAIS OCCASIONAL PAPERS

*America: Images of Empire*, Michael Vlahos (1982), $4.75
*Tilting at Windmills: Reagan in Central America*, Piero Gleijeses, Caribbean Basin Studies Program (1982) (out of print)
*American and European Approaches to East-West Relations*, Robert E. Osgood (1982), $3.95
*A Socialist France and Western Security*, Michael M. Harrison and Simon Serfaty (1981), $4.75

## SAIS REVIEW

Biannual journal of international affairs, $7.00 (subscription prices vary)

To order copies of these publications contact the FPI Publications Program, School of Advanced International Studies, The Johns Hopkins University, 1740 Massachusetts Avenue, N.W., Washington, D.C. 20036 (202-332-1977)/*SAIS Review* (202-332-1975).

# WESTVIEW PRESS/FOREIGN POLICY INSTITUTE

## SAIS PAPERS IN INTERNATIONAL AFFAIRS

1. *A Japanese Journalist Looks at U.S.-Japan Relations*, Yukio Matsuyama (1984), $14.00
2. *Report on Cuba: Findings of the Study Group on United States-Cuban Relations*, Central American and Caribbean Program, ed. (1984), $8.50
3. *Peacekeeping on Arab-Israeli Fronts: Lessons from the Sinai and Lebanon*, Nathan A. Pelcovits (1984), $24.00
4. *The Evolution of American Strategic Doctrine: Paul H. Nitze and the Soviet Challenge*, Steven L. Rearden (1984), $19.50
5. *Nuclear Arms Control Choices*, Harold Brown and Lynn E. Davis (1984), $10.50
6. *International Mediation in Theory and Practice*, Saadia Touval and I. William Zartman (1985), $31.00
7. *Report on Guatemala: Findings of the Study Group on United States-Guatemalan Relations*, Central American and Caribbean Program, ed. (1985), $12.00
8. *Contadora and the Central American Peace Process: Selected Documents*, Bruce Michael Bagley, Roberto Alvarez, and Katherine J. Hagedorn, eds. (1985), $32.00
9. *The Making of Foreign Policy in China: Structure and Process*, A. Doak Barnett (1985), $22.00 (hardcover)/$10.95 (softcover)
10. *The Challenge to U.S. Policy in the Third World: Global Responsibilities and Regional Devolution*, Thomas Perry Thornton (1986), $30.00
11. *Defending the Fringe: NATO, the Mediterranean, and the Persian Gulf*, Jed C. Snyder (forthcoming)
12. *Fiscal and Economic Implications of Strategic Defenses*, Barry M. Blechman and Victor A. Utgoff (1986), $22.75
13. *Strategic Defense and the American Ethos: Can the Nuclear World Be Changed?* Michael Vlahos (1986), $15.00
14. *The Soviet Union and Ballistic Missile Defense*, Bruce Parrott (1987)

To order copies contact Westview Press, Customer Service Department, 5500 Central Avenue, Boulder, CO 80301 (303-444-3541). All prices are subject to change and do not include postage. VISA and MasterCard accepted.

# SAIS

VOLUME 7, NUMBER 1
WINTER–SPRING 1987

# REVIEW

## THE POLITICS OF TERRORISM

Building an Antiterrorist Consensus
**GEORGE BUSH**

The Uses and Abuses of Terrorism
**GARY G. SICK**

The Reagan Doctrine: Containment's Last Stand?
**ROGER D. HANSEN**

Israel: Politics and the Peace Process
**SAMUEL W. LEWIS**

The PLO: Peace or Self-Preservation?
**AARON DAVID MILLER**

Hussein's Constraints, Jordan's Dilemma
**ARTHUR DAY**

Reagan and the Middle East
**MARTIN INDYK**

## *MORE THAN A JOURNAL, A RESOURCE!*